The beauty of these poems will carry you

through the book joyfully.

The skill in thought and word-crafting will bring you

back again and again.

This is a book you will be proud to share with others.

Come start your journey...

AMERICAN SCREAM
PALINDROME APOCALYPSE

AMERICAN SCREAM
PALINDROME APOCALYPSE

by Dubravka Oraić Tolić

OOLIGAN PRESS
PORTLAND STATE UNIVERSITY

American Scream: Palindrome Apocalypse
by Dubravka Oraić Tolić

ISBN: 1-932010-10-6
       978-1-932010-10-7

Translation by Sibelan Forrester, William E. Yuill, and Sonja Bašić.
Revision by Julienne Eden Bušić.
Cover photo by Miroslav Šutej, *Covered eyes* (Prekrivene oči, 2004).
Cover design by Kevin "Vinnie" Kinsella.

This publication is the product of Ooligan Press and the Publishing
Program of the Center for Excellence in Writing at Portland State
University. It was produced entirely by the students of this program. For
credits, see acknowledgments.

Publication of this work is partially underwritten by a grant
from the Ministry of Culture of the Republic of Croatia.

Portions of this book were previously published in the Croatian
language.

Your **free enhanced version** of this
book is at www.enhancedbooks.com!
Visit today.

193☐ 201☐ 01☐ 06

Ooligan Press
Center for Excellence in Writing
Department of English
Portland State University
PO Box 751
Portland, OR 97207-0751
ooligan@pdx.edu
www.publishing.pdx.edu

CONTENTS

PREFACE

Incentive for the translation of my poetry into English came from the American Slavist, Sibelan Forrester, who was studying in Zagreb, Croatia, and became interested in my poem, *American Scream*. In the early 1990s she began to translate the poem with the intention of releasing the translation on the occasion of the 500-year anniversary of Columbus' discovery of America (1492–1992). Meanwhile, the war which shook this part of Europe at that time prevented us from realizing our plan.

This edition includes two long poems: the English version of *American Scream* (*Urlik Amerike*, 1981) and the bilingual, Croatian-English version of *Palindrome Apocalypse* (*Palindromska apokalipsa*, 1993). *American Scream* differs from the original Croatian version in that it contains several new texts and a new order to the poems. Both poems are accompanied by self-commentaries. I provided a commentary to the poem *American Scream* in a fictional letter to the United States Ambassador to Croatia, Peter W. Galbraith, written in 1994. It was published in *Perspectives on Modern Central and East European Literature: Quests for Identity* (Todd Patrick Armstrong, Editor, Palgrave, 2001). A shorter version is published here. A commentary on *Palindrome Apocalypse* has been included in this book in the form in which it was written in 1992, and published in Croatian in 1993.

My deepest gratitude to Sibelan Forrester for the love and patience she has shown to my verses throughout all these years. I also thank Sanja Matešić for valuable touches from a Croatian reader's point of view, William E. Yuill for providing answers to my many questions, Bernarda Katušić for her close reading of my poetry, and Sonja Bašić for some last suggestions before sending out this manuscript to the publisher. My sincere thanks also go to my teaching assistant Danijela Lugarić, on this side of the ocean, and project manager Beth Dillon and senior editor David Cowsert, on the other side, who by exchanging e-mails back and forth with the speed of light so capably resolved the many technical questions. Special thanks go to Julienne Eden Bušić for initiating and guiding the project to its end, and finally, my publisher Dennis Stovall, and Ooligan Press for their efforts to publish poetry in these prosaic times.

Dubravka Oraić Tolić, Zagreb, April 2005

AMERICAN SCREAM

translated by Sibelan Forrester

Too many nights awake and wakings
At dawn. Conquistadores change
Their attire, but their nature
Never

Poets are Indians. Verses
Reservations

You need not struggle for poems
Just as for death

∻ After the verses of Croatian poet, Antun Branko Šimić (1898–1925): "Poets are a wonder in the world."

1   America has a smiling face
    And always arrives with the best intentions
    Usually in spring, when the mayflowers flower
    Of sailors and seas. When you want to vomit
    From the waves on shore
    And when old shores are short

America comes in the name of the freest freedom
    With a subtext of ivory. And frees
    For the happy exploitation of whiteness

America is like dialectics
    A cry lies in it just as dialectics
    Hold I, and sky, and die

America is the fear and trembling
    Of stranded poets

Poets, with broken ribs
    Lie in the sand:
    In blood of poems

    And the shores shorten

2

The ideal of grandfathers, decanted into the blood of sons
A dream of beauty, health, plenty
The East attacks
From the flank

At the eastest place, *O sword from the sheath, brethren*
Where the East instead of grain offers ideas
Where the cities are poorer, lower, narrower
But the punks wonderful and sorrowful just like the good guys

Wretched East!
Here gold is polished to red-hot steel
Here worms themselves leap beneath the teeth of the righteous
Here winds blow through the soul

O joyous destiny of the poet!
All differences are past
Rejoice in this shipwreck
Of democracy and shoes of bast

:~ Citation from the opera *Nikola Šubić Zrinski* (1876) by Croatian composer and
conductor Ivan Zajc (1832–1914).

~ If between me and India there stands an equal sign, then I shall never get to live. Like Zeno's arrow, I shall remain without life, for if I were to live, some difference would have to exist, and if a difference were to exist, some one of us, of India and me, would have to be dead, and if one of us is dead, then life for that one is definitely lost, and if life is definitely lost for someone who is equal to someone, then the other one too is lost, etc., etc.

HOME IS GONE, THE ROAD IS DONE
And a new distance
Swallows its
Son

3

~ The aporia of the Greek philosopher Zeno of Elea, in which an arrow that has been shot remains stationary in spite of its movement.

4

Yellow and indigo seas of force
Seas of murders, seizure by nightmares and seas
:~ But why? *Quare? Pourquoi? Wozu? Zachem?*

For the black grain of pepper pounded to the ground
For the parched pelt of a battered beaver
For the hot blood drop of a carved cup of tea
For a dozen dreamily disembarking women
For home, for king
For the sting
Of ashen-grey novelty

Which, O well-earned spite
Opens its jaws to bite
The head off pilgrim
And path

Our India, who art mislaid
In the clouds that shroud the newest Columbi
America, why is it that you
Issue from out of my mouth?

:~ *quare* (Latin), *pourquoi* (French), *wozu* (German), *zachem* (Russian)—why.

5

> The shore of delight
> Recedes from sight
> Ships sail the ocean
> And water in motion

Sea weed. Indigo and violet threads, fingers stretch into the water, under the water. A bird is not familiar with horror when it catches sight of a fish between the algae. Nor the child who for the first time, t h e   f i r s t t i m e goes into the cold, clear water inundated with weeds. How tiny are the boats with all cargoes in the indigo eyes of underwater beauties. Who is the one to place and erase the signs, the heaps of signs, between the seaweeds, birds, and the boats that seek unfound happiness.

They say that Columbus recognized the coast of India by the algae. Yes, it really was a coast. But the algae said nothing else. Sea weeds are not guilty for the blood that here, look, trickles down the stars.

How many little, utterly little people tonight for the first time felt their own, t h e i r   o w n water between their legs?

6

There are no more maids
The fine's no longer paid
The gold is produced
The sky is used

There are fewer and fewer bitter enemies
The steadfast lost property
For the benefit of the majority which quickly foliates
Into utilizable individuals

Units of new individuals
Ideas and gold reconciled
Russia got red-hot
My "therefore" is reviled

And Magnitogorsk is ever more bitter
Magnet gore or gorgeous mage

7   This world has a big moustache
       Frightful
       This age-old continent
       Honorably slackens
       Before the raging binge to which things have come
       At the expense of one captain's breakdown

       This world carries
       The cerebral convolutions of its head
       To motley conquistadores' marketplaces
       And hangs in each house
       New
               Now already moustached
                          :~   Madonnas above the bed

:~ Allusion to the *Mona Lisa* with a moustache by Marcel Duchamps and to Stalin's portrait in family homes in the Eastern bloc.

8

Old Europe is migrating
Beneath Columbus' tattered mast
Hairy chests buzz
Hunched thunders of the past

Classics bellow in the bowels of boats
Stuffed full of insatiability
Sailors stare into distances
And think of preserves

Gentlemen, monuments are little use
But as decoration fine to choose
Boats multiply cargoes with fish and crusts
The fish are just as mute as busts

You haven't seen India here, I trust?

9

It's easiest to discover America
Then later run aground on its brownish roar
And to establish cities which will forget
The best dreams of their establishers
Dreamt in pale April, chilly May

But all Americas are nice
Brutal, black, and too clean
Like a bitter glass of spice
With Americas what can you mean?

For Americas are always more important than you
For they drive you to lie
And wipe themselves with the papers of your truths

~ WHOEVER IS FOR AMERICA, PLEASE SAY AYE!

~ Reference to the cliché used at open votes in Communist countries. Failure to agree
to the conclusions put forward, i.e. failure to say "Aye" (or raise one's hand) revealed
who the "enemies of the people" were.

India
I bite you
India
Golden Poisoned
Apple

10

Enormous candies hover
Above my acid face
Or children are no longer barefoot
Or there is no wine, no food

Roulettes, couplets, bracelets
Pierre, please, dis-moi la vérité...
Noch einmal, eshcho raz, once more
What land is this again, Peter

And where is our door?

:~ *Roulettes, couplets, bracelets*: wordplay with French; *dis-moi la vérité* (French), tell me
the truth; *noch einmal* (German); *eshcho raz* (Russian), once more.

1 1

From this shore begins a new pain
And for the hundredth time my love is put on ice. From my
Best discoveries flow a honey that isn't. They make houses of the eyes
Of plants found by chance and of cattle. They erect golden barns
For the new cattle, golden greenhouses for exotic flora
Of the newest varieties. And orators flick like the tongues of just created
Water factories. For nothing is important while the lip is sufficiently
Damp that the poison sucked from a Persianly provoked weed
Pours, while new nations swarm, and the old
Sweat. And children already know that better words come from the
Word "Beat" and run into the word "battle" with a ring
Of artificial smoke on their backsides. What they are permitted
They instead of their fathers, potential former
Columbi who meanwhile teach other people's children the shiniest
Principles in the shiniest gardens of love of justice
Or the justice of love
∴ Through history and a brighter future into justice and freedom
Onward

Each shore is less new
For the pain is the same

∴ Ideological cliché from the Communist period.

12

An upright rod
A neck bent
And the wrong road
And a thief by strength

A wind-swine
Serenity terrorizes
A pair of socks with no legs
Sweeps into paradises

1 3

Invisible land
Amidst the map

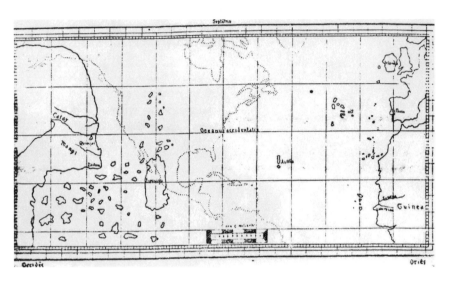

A reconstruction of Toscanelli's map, dating from 1474

This world is not new
Columbus is Odysseus
America—a siren
And we are hostages all
On the road to Ithaca
WHAT AN IRRESISTIBLE CALL!

Frightful land
Land of fear
Divided into whites and blacks
And one other land also divided
But into red and rose
And a third, and a fourth
And land after land
All equal and in very similar poses
Far and near
Lands of the earth's sphere

And one Christopher
Amid the sea

And one India
Out of reach

And one picture
Like this:

Night of fierceness
Christ. Affair
Of water on the cross
And cross on the water

14

15
Frightful island
700 houses 300 residents
One church no priest
One girl 298.5 old women
And 0.5 fisherman
Who at night pounds the squid
Shoes of wool
Not one olive
Not one pine
And all on the sea
Houses, stone sugar
Frightful island
Island of fright
Frightfulness itself
Floats amidst the sea

:~   The ship "Ivan Gundulić"
:~:~   — *Was ist auf der Insel zu sehen?*
Reed amidst the sea
A white graveyard: gingerbread belly
Everywhere the battle for bread goes on
Somewhere in America
2000 people
Are there authorities on the island?
Excommunicated community
On the wall: "Power to the people!" Red
Erased by the winds
The main thing is the bar: BROADWAY, pr.
Johnny Lister, but it's not open
The wind imparts a part to my hair
Not a cup of tea
Anywhere

Leeward. Sun. How warm it is
January
Si parla italiano. Really

:~ Ivan Gundulić, the Croatian Baroque poet (1589–1638).

:~:~ (German), "What is there to see on the island?

18

Don't sappiamo che we are
My father's Greek, and I'm Austrian
Children Italian, Yugoslav
Croatian?
∶~ *Ma che nonsense!*
And expertly gathers up her
Hundred-year mourning
Black through the wind
Into the wind

Wind
Boats rammed into the flank of the
Shore
There are tourists
Winter
∶~∶~ — *Was für eine Insel, Katarina?*
So tot, so furchtbar
Sea, dead pond
No sign of a sailor
Just
Here and there
A frozen fish
On a frozen beach
And scaling this year's urchins

~∶   A SNACK OF SUSAK

~ In the original text, a pidgin mixture of Croatian and Italian: "Here Italian is
   spoken," "We don't know who we are," "What nonsense!"

∶~∶~ (German), "What kind of island is this, Catherine? / So dead, so terrible."

~∶ Susak, a Croatian island in the northern Adriatic. Most of its inhabitants left for
   America in the great wave of emigration in the early twentieth century.

16

All is Ithaca
Ithaca is all
Ithacas are like that
And in no way different
Fevered eaves
Sheaves of fear
Shore and sham
Ithacas are all:
Both sea
And Homer
And Odysseus
Islands
Eyes of land

And what if India is
The white and clean
Ground of Ithacas
From which grows
The darkness of Americas

17

India isn't Indiana
In India there's no Pakistan nor Mudjibur Rahman
India's neither a whole continent, nor all continents together
India's not to the right, to the left, nor in the center
Neither is India salvation in Marx
Nor is India Marx in salvation

In India there truly are people how many there truly are
In India it's truly winter if it's truly winter
By all its very best qualities
India has escaped from hell, my reader

Neither circle nor line
Neither line nor circle

Poets aren't comrades aunties
                         always to have to sew up something

1 8

America is not the United States
And doesn't occupy 9,363,123 km² and doesn't have
221,895,548 inhabitants
America is not *Mountains* with the chiseled visages
               of Washington, Jefferson, Roosevelt and Lincoln
Nor Niagara Falls nor the biggest automobile factory in Detroit
America is not the *Declaration of Independence* of 1776
Nor the president killed in the theater
Nor the president killed in Dallas

We are all America
Wherever we may be
Whatever we do

America is what is born
From our dreams without our knowing
America is what happens to us
On the way to Indias:

Our daily bread
Which we discover and discover
Following
               INDIADNA'S THREAD

19

Head to head, and not a one smiling
Woman to woman, and not a one loved
Man to man, and not a one proud

And the orphaned orphanages of love
In which the leprous lip of Eros
Goes on a spree

> Stone structures spread their white threads
> Towards the gloom of the future

But maybe America is this too: 20
Scream to scream and again anew
New! New! New!
The very newest new,
          my good man
America's the way you multi-plan

> *There's no doubt, you are right:*
> *The stars are Indies that shine at night*

Meanwhile
Or the Vladivostok of
eternity

The bastards multiply violently   **21**
Between power and money
Too often black night falls
And I'm too often funny

The wolves become members
The villagers die out
Winter and death gradually disappear
Summer becomes the goal
Of faithful unbelievers

It's morning, and Croatia must seek the sea
Like Vladivostok the vulture and shock

The Ark of Arcadia
Irresistibly sails on

22

∴ O beloved, O dear, O sweet America
Of the long-haired Croatian madonna now singing
Very charmingly palmed off. With the knife
Of salvation. But very, very well-disposed, for disposition isn't
Hair, while hair is always hair and is not changed, but
Changes. Frightfully dialectically changes
Indias every fifth spring

When the accessories of the spring
Wardrobe change
And when my friends
Are led away, spat on and robbed
Robbed, spat on and led away

To the newest water factories

> *Let each thing bring into the ring*
> *Old and young bring into the ring*
> *The ring, the ring, Americ, anemic*
> *Ring, etc.*

∴ A citation from the pastoral play *Dubravka* by Ivan Gundulić: "O beloved, O dear, O sweet [freedom]."

One more pace steps into eternity
Steps, O steps and states

The rabble wrapped in fear
Blusters through shining cities
And purchases and spends
Its unearned cents

Only stone is still broken
By hand in special teams
Otherwise plastic's now the token
Indestructible as a scream

23

East-West
Or then this
way

Not step by step
New lands are found
On this water
Boats run aground

Europe, puffed up like a frog
In the cornfields of American skyscrapers
That devour the air

24

Irrigated toilers
Dehydrated wells
The West works on the East
The East works on the West

∻ *Und ewig rollt das Rad*
OF AMERICA
                multiplied

∻ A citation from Friedrich Nietzsche: "And the wheel [of Being] keeps eternally rolling."

25

A Scream of Dream

America of this poem
Is not THAT America
THIS America wasn't discovered by Columbus really sailing
But by us—cringing to riches and power
Amerigo Vespucci only described Columbus' discovery
THIS discovery was signed by our heart and mind
        As a kind
        Of innocent, absolute climb
THAT America was destroyed by the conquistadores
So that all future descendants would build it in their present
THIS one was moved by conquistadores into the future
So as to prevent any present
THAT America immediately grasped
What India is and where
THIS one will live and die in the faith
That it is India itself
And that, besides Itself, there is
No India

Loathsome brood
Of naked days
History multiplied
Rides back over the waves

Spirit of India
Over the waters of America
Like smoke
Over factories

In the rosy cut of fear, in the fever
Of free facts of dawns and seas
The noisy crack:
"BREAD AND BREAK!"

And we belch out
Into the tight
Inseverable
Embrace
            of cranes
                    and khans

26

27

And I hear the roar:
CATCH UP AND OVERTAKE AMERICA
(The masses erupt into salvation)

To shove with the word "HURRAH" for a crust of bread
Is a matter of a morsel or else of a reason
When the stars darken, and God disappears
The blood of paradise is worse still than the red color of hell

How great
The Kulikovo fields
We are that will
For a better god
Willing to kill
Rolling in blood

Cities, water, time
A glance is ice
And everyone stops
And everything clots
Unknown question mark
My frozen scream
It is indigo hordes
Traversing us

28

In the best land
Or India's happy end

In the best land the living is best
All the problems are laid to rest
In the best forests the best birds nest
Of all the ages this is the best

In this best land it's best to be
A citizen approximately
Beloved of rivers, swung to and fro
By the wind, you look from on all below
The superstructure above, below you the basis
There is no desert without an oasis

Your teachers repose in peace
On the best wall, in the best frame
And now they rejoice for you and for me
In satisfied, happy, red-cheeked fame

The next day or
India
Sing me thy
~ *Anger*

From the topmost forehead troops race
Minutes spill from the eyes
From the horse's lip, from the Asiatic face
Each uniformed hour flies

The times of the Huns on the clock's hands
Battered meetings flee away
Enormous fur-coated Attila stands
To grab me from the first entryway

29

~ Allusion to Homer's *Iliad*. On the day the Croatian Spring was crushed,
  1 December 1971, mounted police rode into the main square in Zagreb, and
  military troops stood by in nearby streets. Other republics of former Yugoslavia
  also sent military reinforcements.

30

The brief autobiography of one Indian woman
(In the early seventies of the twentieth century)

On the bread of democratization I husk my greyed teeth
The whiteness of my legs speaks of a darkness that is never spoken of
But I do not fear
Hairiness is a signum of turbulent classes
My legs are white, without hairs
Through them flows imprisonment
I am like that

Through the window I see the town like blood and banner
Through the bars
Along a street I cannot identify
Leaderless people dance as syrup
They gave all of themselves
I did not do so well
Therefore instead of legs I have crutches
For I am like that

∾ From a shack in Mala Mlaka to a palace in Topeka
It's not the farthest trip
All bricks are dangerous
But still I do not fear
Anyone
It's good that there's no more Dear God
Perhaps I would fear him
I am loyal
And like that

An enormous drum does its job
∾∾ Some sort of dwarves dash through the SQUARE
I'm from the beloved clique so they let me on the SKYSCRAPER

∾ A village near Zagreb.

∾∾ The verses describe the demonstrations on Republic Square (now Ban Jelačić
   Square) in Zagreb, December 1971, when the Croatian Spring was suppressed.

34

And I freely
With all my nails Scrape Sky
I know it's not pretty
But a necessity
At any rate
When I'm like that

Yesterday a tram bit me on the leg
All that I had to shriek, I did it long ago
I preferred to limp off to the UNIVERSITY and Learn the Universe
It was marvelous
No one was spiteful or long-legged
Everyone had legs again
And even I had them
That way I am

And the way that I am like is very undifferentiable
Indeed low-toned like a locomotive pipe in a basement
Where my vampired mind glassily pleases
Someones of the most touching ancestry
To whom I belong and write in their way
While to me one altogether
Largest and greyed
— Mouse, rat?
Crutch the air from the lungs

— But w h a t   are you saying?

I say

      The road to India
      Is paved with Indians
      America's stones
      Rest on their bones
            Everything is trampled
            The wind writes out in golden letters:
        :~ *"Don't indtouch my circles!"*

:~ Alludes to the saying of the Greek mathematician Archimedes. When, after the conquest of Syracuse in 212 B.C., he was attacked (and perhaps killed) by a Roman soldier while he was drawing geometric figures in the sand, he said, "*Noli turbare circulos meos*" (Don't disturb my circles).

3 1

O comrade Circle
But you have no shadow
But you are already
A new line

That night in the Bolkonskins' house
:~ *No one was sleeping*
Everyone saw the indigo disappearance of the dark
Everyone looked at the blue loss of the dim beam
Everyone stared at the bluish overcoming of points
Of themselves and all their relatives
At the growing up of a great, universal
Communal
And snow-white
Mausoleum of Dawn

I live in circles that spread
Through new centuries
And old nights

Point my point
Tiniest India

:~ From Leo Tolstoy's *War and Peace.*

32

(View from below)
That turbid Copernican
That yellow American
That morning in Newtoning
That Newtoning through to bottom
∿ *Evenings at Christophernanda's*
Those hard hard aquabuses
Breads of the Inds

IN A HUNCHBACKED NIGHT
QUASIMODO KISSES
HIS WONDROUS INDIA

(View from above)
Our spines are ornate
In the name of India
In the name of America
            We
                  Grate
                              (Gather?)
                                          Fate

∿ Alludes to the title of Nikolai Gogol's *Evenings at Dikanka.*

33

And what are we
And what is India
Pictures belch out
Of working legends

In mornings which are mornings since they are mornings
When we drink paradise tea, eat bread, when
We dash, everything's fast, but it's done hurriedly
In haste, and sixteen longitudinal and sixteen transversal
Indias cut through the heart
Through blood and fog, through fog and plan
And from our sweaty Indian flesh, from our
White Sea that we're constructing
And reconstructing
From all that we are for
We are
Emerges our very own, wet America
And a new, the newest
Day, comrades, can with good reason begin to grow
And only grow
Towards
Evening

It's good that there is evil
It's evil that there is good
With a strong step continues
The withering away of the stars

34   *Relations, relations, relations*
                     Themselves

Although he in fact kept emphasizing that this was in fact a matter
Of a path like any path and that India was
Everywhere and nowhere. But no one believed and everyone thought
That he had discovered something and was now deftly concealing that
            Something with some sort of
Reddish excuses such as a path like any path. And the helm would
Become a flagpole. That bothered him terribly, but he did not want to
Show it so as not to show his nonexit. With all those more or less red
Monsters that were nevertheless in connection with him. And he in fact
            Had something to do with it.
With all those transversal railroads through hearts. For he isn't
Innocent of everything either. For he couldn't sail on his own. For with
Salt alone you can't measure the pain that devours you somewhere in the
            Inside and therefore he needed
Sailors

Sailors sailors
Your watery salary
Hits the dry land
Of the stiffened sea

Ship towards ship
Let's sing, let's sing the water
And gigantic lasses with knives
Of the newest salvation in agitated minds
And the bravery to slit open a cloud to plug up a mouth
To enrich the rabble
And the silt called dollar dinar rouble
Let us sing

                              O reverse
                              Food's flowing
                              I seeping into India
                              India out of me going

39

35

MY IND-YORK
(school of a dream
scrape of a scream)

TEACHER: Tell me, please, the genitive nominative of the nominative genitive of the normal indom drilled yesterday into an adverb, and write on the indoard (legibly, legibly, so we can all see through!) this inveterate indivicity of ours.

PUPIL: Now—knew...

TEACHER: And now what would be the definition of America?

PUPIL: The land of dreams which every day begins with screams.

TEACHER: Excellent and bravo! Just continue this way. And I, your indol, can say now from my whole heart:

∻ INDIPIT, INDIPIT INDA NOVA. Look, look, why the sun confirms it too!

From the sheath the penetration
Of atmospheric swords
Pettinute celestial sand
And a word that squeezes song
To an entirely second-hand gong

∻ Wordplay with the Latin saying: "Incipt vita nova."

40

36

Indapitalism: An Indo-American indation indacterized by the relation of free Columbus and the indapitalist. Columbus is free insomuch as he is not the property of anyone, but is also, in order to maintain life, compelled to sell his travel resources on the sea. The owner of indiquid means—the indapitalist—purchases his travel resources for a specified traveling period. Since Columbus travels more than his travel resources are paid, he creates an indapitalistic surplus of path and thus enables the indacumulation of indapital and expinded indaproduction. Indacteristic of inderal indapitalism was the indacurrence of indapital, which consequently saw large indapitalists indisposing small ones, and afterwards also a hyperindruction of indoods, which latter led to inderior indicrises and finally to indwar. Towards the end of the twentieth century appeared the indeation of great indopolies and the indestruction of indastrial and indancial indapital. In this inderiod, the inderiod of inderialism, indicative are indasterial indcrease of indicial indapital as well as indespotic indapital. The newest indase in the indevelopment of indapitalism is indacterized by the phenomenon of postindapitalism, in which Columbus becomes conscious of himself and of the Indimerican indation as such. On the occasion of the 500th anniversary of his discovery of America, in 1992, Columbus realizes that he has discovered not India, where he had headed, but something quite different, and that this discovery leads to the fundamental indisquention of the indapitalistic manner of proinduction and the sole indeology of indoculture.

~ Wordplay with the root *ind* and the name of Columbus, modeled after the lexicographic centre "Capitalism" from the *Filozofski rječnik* (*Dictionary of Philosophy*, Zagreb, 1965, pp. 200-201).

41

37

One more indefinition

America—the land between reality and dreams
And our estates grow less and less
And greater and greater is
American happiness
A SACK THAT LACKS SEAMS

India—EMERGENCY EXIT
What a crowd!

38

       :~   *Indienation, its end and its*
              Rested beginning

Every morning we raise
Every evening we lower
All four americas
By the front americas we rush forward
By the hind americas we rush backward
And right at the apex of our rose sun
And our powdery pain that frightfully divides
And our cereal happiness mixed with bees' milk
And one overly high Everything
In the lulls of hunched Nothing
Of violet agriculture
We'll no longer go through the sea of ears
But through the plough-fields of the sea
And all of us through all and everything
We'll bravely cast off the wasted hullusters
Correctly and greyishly
We'll open both americas wide
Beginning to pour the last battle of the eye
In the name of wrong so it would be put right
In the name of sight so it would be giant
So it awes and so it saw
Now this now that
But always the same
Without doubt of how
Broad
      Boundless
                Plains
                        (of Poles?)
Become
       A new
                Better
                    Sea

:~ Reference to the word *alienation*, a key term in Marxist ideology.

Effect of open seas. Repose of the fact:
Three-fourths of the sphere of the body
And three-fourths of the earthly sphere
Are
Watery Jesuses

Today this, tomorrow that
Land

Here can be found the howl of the waves
Here can be found a map of the sea and a ripped belly
Here can be found a whole people here shore and boat
Here we can be found and our
Fathers and bones altogether a billion
The last prince of the last princes
Here all and together a costly number
Heavy the cargo of humanity
At the eternal place without breath
Stingy and sacred laborers shoulder
The heavy "NO!" of laborers' callouses
With the strong brisk powerful voice
Of morning uprisings and eight hours
Of the revolting sea named work
Which will gladden us some day
Here close as brothers racially passionately
Lovers always of Better
Accumulated class palisades
Here harmony commits arson
And the young INDIGENIUS
Offers a motive to the Wind

39

AND WHAT DID SIGHT TELL US THEN
≁ AND WHAT DID GIANT TELL US THEN
It was high time
To throw into the sea's

Jaws

A new

Share

Of shore

≁ Sight and giant are in the Croatian palindromic: *Vid i div.*

40

:~ *Many attractive possibilities*

Many attractive possibilities of India which is not EITHER-OR, of India which is NOT ONLY BUT ALSO, India which stands in **AB** vis-à-vis **A**, in **A** vis-à-vis—**A**, in **B**, in **C**, in **D**, in a good infinity assisted by unprecedented liveliness. Well we're finally getting under the very skin of the earth! O fruitful shores, O respected stars! *Embracing. Universal embracing. Encirclement without encirclement, bud without rose, rose without bush, prison without son, shiver in the sun, on the summit,* and we are freezing, freezing ourselves.

And picture after picture, after picture picture, for the benefit of our youth which we defend, and shall defend, from age.

> *The wheel is ours*
> *We are wheels*
> *Who in it and who in us*
> *Pours out his frozen bloody salvation*

:~ Wordplay with clichés of Marxist and Socialist ideology.

41

It's not India, but Indies
Sea my sea
You beat hard in the heart

Description of the sky
Starry eruption
Powdering of Indies
With ashes of Americas

INDICENT! INDICENT!
The maniac whetted his heels on the water
With overly wet
Consequences

And what is happening?

For from now to us
Through the main hole in the breast
In shape watery blue and salty
Flows out the methane of happy Etnas

:~ Alludes to the novel *From Here to Eternity* by James Jones.

Homer ate up the Iliad
And vomited the Odyssey
Whoever has been once to Hades
Will always try to fly

42   Comrades, what a sea!
Comrades, what tempests!
Comrades, what vessels!
That's the past!
For it's we that are the sea
For it's we that are the tempests
For it's we that are the vessels
India—that is you:
Your used youth

And we rotate, rotate
Around the stars

        America

            And death

From here to the sand
Sea after sea strand
Celestial innkeepers
Wet are your dollars

43

∿ *Solstice*

The sun had already leapt up high. There were lots of people. Birds circled in the air lit up by the sun's rays. The birds linked the people into one thought, which was linking them. There were really a lot of people. They were all the youngest people. And they thought something and wanted something.

But when a man arrived in a shortish tunic, a markedly shaggy fur cap impaled on trenchantly flashing eyes, and in sturdy cloth pants which on the one hand gave away the sturdy character of the stranger, while on the other they plunged first of all into hand-knitted woolen socks and later, if we turn—which neither is nor can be amiss—our glance lower, into shoes not only waterproof, but no doubt coarse, though resistant to any misfortune and therefore entirely practical, adjusted the thick scarf which served him as a trustworthy or certain defense against even the bitterest cold and frost, and he cried out at the top of his voice on that clear day:

"BOYS AND GIRLS, AREN'T YOU THIRSTY?"

∿ The poem stylizes a cliché used by socialist agitators appearing in public before the masses of the younger generation who were to be reeducated in the revolutionary spirit.

Water our water
Why are you so
Sought-after

44   Shore to shore shore
Sea to sea sea
Someone spake: "We came!"
Someone added: "A shame!"

And enormous merriment breaks
Through the hot lips of America
The icy-cold taste of
INDI-COLA

What refreshment
For traveling in place

45

> :~ *Back sonnies of America*
> *That way can also be right*
> *Dawns are eternally roses*
> *They must be plucked from night*

One and the same thing everywhere
Everywhere finding of the unfindable
Everywhere research of the unsearchable
Everywhere destructions within reach of home
Everywhere Americas nowhere India

Columbus Columbus
Your 1492 became for me 1492
Eternities and one symbol

Of a watery cross because not even a poem can spare itself
From crossness and the crossicity of the world in general
Only the winds are free and hats in the sea
1492 eternities
Shall eternally indate
For their murmur

> *Don't gogolate, madman not a one*
> *For if there truly is gold*
> *Then it is*
> *Silence*

Time is no longer time
But the moment of a poem
In the yellow perhaps smiling discrepancy
Between India and America

:~ Allusion to the beginning verses of the *Marseillaise*.

46

journalistic, I

On Lang Square, in Zagreb, in the parking lot, the MADMAN of Gogol's DIARY has been found. Smallish in stature, with pronounced cheekbones, in blue jeans *(but were there really jeans in Gogol's time?)*, he did pose as a direct descendant of Columbus, which provoked the indignation of citizens. He assured the people that the end of America had come and that the Son of India was born. Smearing himself with gasoline from a nearby pump, he demanded that passersby bow before him. By the hasty action of the organs of persecution the imposter was brought to a nearby public security station, where he is now being held. Teams of experts have immediately become involved in investigating this deplorable incident. We must report with regret that the incident occurred in our city at the very moment when our agriculture achieved a record crop of 181 mc. per hectare and when the traditional friendship with the government and peoples of India and America (recently not excluding even Spain!) has reached its pinnacle of 11,578 meters (for comparison let us recall that the highest summit on earth, which is not by chance located precisely in the immediate vicinity of one of the above-mentioned lands, amounts to 8,882 meters, which is a shortfall in comparison to superior exertions).

ALL FOR INDIA, INDIA FOR ALL

47

journalistic, II

Strong abatements were noticed yesterday on the veins of antediluvian amphibians. Urgent measures should be undertaken, for every delay would mean an irreparable impoverishment of our, the American economy, the economy of a most beautiful, a most rich, a most free land of ecological waterground.

WARNING:
The malachite of goodness
Is digging trenches for its
Young

48

televisionistic, I

ANNOUNCER: Pay attention! The question reads: Who was Columbus? NOW!

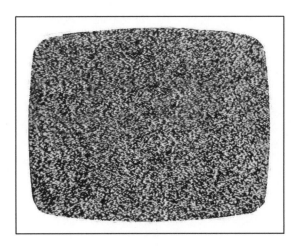

REPLIES
    FALL
        OUT OF THE DARKNESS:
EQUAL
    FLIES
       IN THE MILK
          OF OUR TIMES

49

televisionistic, II

India? But no, comrades, we won't let ourselves be led onto thin ice. I know what is going on. It is the famous circumnavigation of the world that was carried out by Columbus with his comrades. I also know the year, if necessary. Let the commission evaluate my answer. This is a modern TV-QUIZ, and there can be no unscientific manipulation. I have evidence, famous experts are here, you can't convince me. America is a result of the path to India, but no, no, I ask that my answer be valorized and evaluated fairly, comrades, gentlemen, I'm participating on an equal footing in a humane TV-QUIZ and I have the right to a replay, it's all written down, there are millions of witnesses, I'm the father of three children and there's no way I'll let myself be led onto thin ice, this is a modern TV-QUIZ and...

MORE AND MORE
FASTER AND FASTER
THE SCREEN TOTTERS
FROM LETTERS OF WATER

Young Indians
You have to have to
Plough this sea
Of liberty

50

Conversation with the stars

A song carry
The star
It has many points
It is called
MULTIPOINT

FIVEPOINT
Come down already once from that forehead
Find already once another God
The forehead would bravely want
Wish and be allowed
To become the unwrinkled
Sky of eye

White days, dark nights
Why do you alternate
O vision of the Whole
How when where with whom
O Ears
:~ Of the walls

Come on, don't spill that big-eyed blood
There's nothing worse than when something
Freezes like a star

:~ Refers to the saying, "Even the walls have ears."

5 1

Star of Bethlehem
∽   *Or India according to Matthew*
(First fall beneath the picture)

That night, behold, the Magi caught sight of a star in the East. And they departed towards the star. And lo, the star they had seen at its emergence went before them, till it came and stood over where the young Child was. When they saw that the star was going no further, the Magi rejoiced with exceeding great joy. They knew: their path was correct, they were at the right place. And when they were come into the house, they found the young Child with Mary his mother, and they fell down, and worshipped him, and opened their treasures and presented unto him gold, frankincense and myrrh. And being warned of the star in a dream that they should not return to Herod, the Magi departed into their own country another way. And the star led the Child's parents into Egypt, into exile. And the star watched from afar the wrath of King Herod, who sent forth, and slew all the male children that were in Bethlehem, from two years old and under. And the star could do nothing. *This is called the Slaughter of the Innocents.*

Afterwards the star also watched the death of i t s child. Its hands were tied in the sky. It was red from shame. Who has eyes, let him see.

And the sons Jesuses
Did not dull
The trip
We are null
∽∽   *Amen. Sleep*

∽ Cited and paraphrased from the Gospel according to Matthew.

∽∽ In the Croatian original, these verses are palindromic: *I nisu sini / Isusi / … / Nas nema / Amen San.*

52

The American alphabet
Emphasizes eyes in the East

a) Lord, why is thy mouth so murky? What noise is it that rises from within? Art thou eating something then? Lord, what kind of crust is it thou holdest in thy teeth?

b) Sonny, it is bread, wonderful and holy, our daily bread spread with TOMORROW. Pray! The lands are salt from the seas, the seas are tired from the lands, and I'm a person, a traveler of a road...

c) *There's no longer a crucified one*
Only the cross exists
And on it the rose
Of profane necessity
                              Which would all of us

d) *Our fate?*
              Retaliation of the stars

And continuous clasp
Through the sign **C**

5 3   Worlds of light, worlds of darkness
            Cloudy summers, ice-cold winters
            And our crucial crossial name
            All in the terrible sign of **C**
            And through the sign **C**
            We raise and lower
            Melancholy subversions
            Of skinny necks
            And when some of us
            Come down with a crash
            It will be a condition
            For coming up another

        Find this sign
            ∾   In the poem of a great Croatian poet
                And it will be the CRUEL Croatian poet
                And will sing the law of clamp, clench, crowd
                And the unceasing clatter of
                                        Climbing

∾ Allusion to Gundulić's verses from the epic *Osman*: "Wheel of fortune spins round
    / spinning without end: / who once was on top is now on the ground, / who once
    was down is climbing up, up to the top!".

59

54

Book of Genesis

C stole **a** and behind the back of **s** pushed to **e**
So that *case* quickly became leafy *course*
From *course* severe *curse* from *curse* light *cars*
From *cars*, *cry* and *cost*
Slightly redful and dreadful
Creep, crackle, crawl
Are three in a series of *cases* in place
The original mother of *case* is *Canaan*
That has always awaited us in the distance
And the father is naked plain **C**
Cross crest crack
Clan and *cleft* are living hairy *case*
Of the terrible tongue of terror
While *crown* is an endless bottomless uncle
The king of spilling
And a tired horrible *crime* comes again
A new, bright *case*
And from new, bright *case*
Would be again gloomy *cry* and *crush* and lots of new
Hard *crimes* and
So into eternity **C**
Terrible fathers are tempered
But what happened and will happen with *case?*
Better for us to know
From the fiction
Of crucifixion

HOW THE *CASE* WAS TEMPERED
(Sketch of an Apocalypse)

The first *Case* was tempered on the cross
The second *Case* retempered the stars
The third *Case* confirmed the circle
And the fourth—then already a cruel globe
Crossed at its own cost
And the cruise became the country's crisis
A cradle for the refreshment of the crowd
And a strong crossway was tempered
Towards the western East   55
Through the ever-more-creepy cut of crust
And clouds clustered through a circle
The *Case* got cold and gets cold
In the crucial cloudiness of cruel courage
Which is crazy and directionless
Clutched through you and us
Prepared to slaughter kilometers
And the clue to Holy *Case* got lost
And the clue condoled and condoled the *Course*
And the tooth of the heavens was corroded
And consternation conquered the cosmos
Quinine was the most confident condiment
Even cabbage condemned
In the cyclic connection of the four **C**
Arises the last crisis
Cups of conflagration
The steel branches of cranes
And the collapse of compasses for the tree of salvation
And the clatter of a cartridge in the treetops of the mind
Branded curls of the circle
Windy horror through each hair
And the book of cyclic closure
A card for *Case* without *course*
C in the distance cries, of course

:~ Christ, Copernicus, Columbus, Kant: all begin with the letter K in Croatian.

61

56

America contains 99 C^n beginning from India in a straight line or just as many expressed in the seas and dry lands right and left upwards and downwards. And in the illuminated collisions of all of us and you which with the same glow kiss roundly are born new and new spheres of new and new us and you and our love and yours swells and grows as far as the incipient dark spheres of pepper of americanized India or indianized darkness from which the universe and the stars already sneeze.

Father Columbus
India mother
America is a bowl
And it will not let itself
Either be held back or hold

Who and what are
Spheres

A sphere is sky and earth   5 7
A sphere is the stars and the universe
And each eye, each ear is a little sphere just like a grain
From a thousand grained spheres arise spheres
Of corn, of which there's never truly enough. And for the sake of
                                        spheres called
Cocoa, coconut, coffee
Columbus found himself in the hell of the sea, coped and grasped
The egg-sphere so that earth in a little would be
Visible to anyone. And he proved the earthly
Sphere at the cost of future, ever smaller but
Ever stronger spheres, and the cannon began
To fling sphere after sphere, and there began to flow
Sweat—the sphere of work and horror
To a person the dearest sphere of the head
Began to spin and is always spinning
As if there's no end to the spinning
And no one ever saw, but everyone already knew
That there also exist smaller, invisible
Spheres of atoms without a
Home

Sphere to sphere without the corner
And there's no home without the atom
And always the same gusts of wind
And always the same "I" on the bullet
Exposed
Cold
Sold

And we are chased
Into the grave into God into zero into 0

$0 + 0 = 0$
And if the icy paradise of Siberia
Takes a thousand zeroes
It is still the null
Of love

It moves so swiftly
That it does not move

58

But both our second and third **E goes**
In order to be Fiery Nothing

Nothing is nothing and always working
Our Nothing works and works
Until forever a good new boat
When suddenly a strong inroad of voice
Awakened into a new spark of salvation
The new Columbus blazed up all in flame
Rearing **C** in a million new countries
Neither dry land of sea nor sea of land
But suddenly an upper sea
Familiar azure or blue ghost
That now has to gleam like us
That now has to feed the black hungry
And work for us and pay tribute to us
In indigo grain in wine of stars
That now must be a true turning point
And cloudless compressed and rain
Along ever ribbier needs
The murmur to extend to rush to meetings with us
The best most beautiful gentlemen of comrades
And the lava of the old sad Win
Of the god of ugliness and death
Surrenders carefully and necessarily
Before the laborious gift
Of legs that chase and chase
Into the ever lively
Dream of such quick spinning
That everything stands still
It's not a question of sweet
But of the sweat of eternal summer
Which goes out on the nose
Of the firm celestial dream

O UGLY UNREST OF THE UNIVERSE
The axis conquers alas!
Antideath on the cross of work
And the gold of new Cyruses
Produces the bitterest of all hungers

5 9

I thou he we you they
Murdered by the bitterest hunger
Under always the same painful sky
With always the same sowing of self
The face of the fields is furrowed furrows
The ploughsible inlaws are plausibly the same
And there'll be a third crucifixion of Christ
Plus a path to the dazzling
New Anew

Our bread is a board
And the board is always hungry
And child after child
Disappears mown by a new world

60

Sorrow of a circle

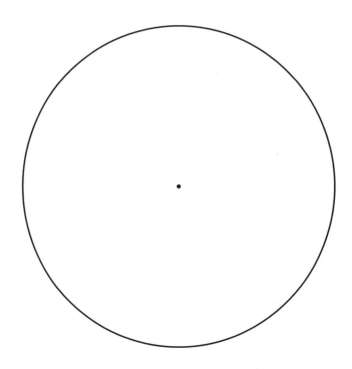

How large are
All Americas
How alone is
Each India

61

With the striped flower of India
In the black buttonhole of America
Killing dust from the shoes
That did kiss the sea

And when my organ that beats
On the left side under the rib
One wonderful day convincingly spake:

Poets can change the world
It's a matter of changing
The poems

I sensed I was no longer sailing anywhere, anywhere
I sensed I was shuddering along my whole body
I sensed I had two ankles
And that I was up to both ankles
In the eternal dilemma of Columbus and of the slime
Of new lands
New horrors
        And I vomit
                without warranties

In the name of the father and of the son
And there's nothing besides the circle
The white white circle
Of high too high
Sky

:~ Paraphrases the idea from Marx's early writings: "Up to now, philosophers have only interpreted the world in different ways; the point however is to change it."

About face left
About face right
And about upon about
Is again a circle

62   There follows an entirely simple cause
One, heaven is overly one
Blue as steel, blue as a blouse
Medusa shines from it instead of the sun

And below the dead fleets future
Rusted through the plough-laps
While tomorrow, brighter and better
Vernally ploughs with the starriest shoulder straps

Poets make seed uselessly thrown
Everywhere only stars are sown

Loud clatter:
Left
    Right
        Left

63

O Lord God, well are there really
No more differences
Differences are no more
And the poem gleams weely

America! America! America!
On you broke the yellow tooth of discovery
All that happened afterwards was again that American
Americanic through plan and misappropriation
Through blood and sacred things Americanesquely
Das amerikanische, americheskoe, ochen'
Ochen' americheskoe

Gold of faith, wind of fraud
And the path through no way and nowhere
The yellow path towards death
There here and back

Yes, *vorwärts* and *vperyod* still lead
But no longer into New
Rather more and more
Into wind, oratory, and gore

⁓ (German and Russian), American, American, very, very American.

⁓⁓ (German and Russian), Onward!

64

The hunchbacked mark of salvation grows up through eternity
In the word. Osiris wakes again in roll-eyed Columbus
Ashamed to the most shameless shame, pounded
Into the pepper of discovery along the shores of the newest
Liquid ivory, while
Somewhere on the horizon stripedly shows blackwhite
Still another (which one in order?) torch that gives life. Columbus
Knew he was also guilty himself, but that guilt is also the criminal, and
Columbus got really confused. He had never been a toady, nor an
ass-kisser nor a conspicuous pan-licker, nor an arch traitor, although he,
It's well known, often licked
Full bowls of abandonment
Just as he used to sit comfortably so as to
Waste away to a bag of bones. A MAN WHO TOOK UP AN EGG
BECAUSE OF THE FORM OF THE EARTH
Though perhaps hands want something else
When the thick drops get too interlaced
And when he would no longer see what way he could go
Today Columbus is madder than yesterday
But that does not astonish him

And had he India truly found
He would never have fooled around
But the fact that ceaselessly instead of It
This way, that way
He always finds new Americas

Each time anew
It comes to Columbus like good thunder for many reasons
But still most of all because no one
Instead of love would accidentally mix him
A bromide and so
Settle him for all centuries

Conspicuously shimmery superdiscoveries
That he's been finding for more than five centuries
Drive him into the grave and drag him back again
And love is his propeller, there's always to be found

A new sweetheart
And new sons constantly fly out

Columbus is not proud of them because he's their father
But because he enjoys the process
Process
Of Love

COlumbO
That sounds so **C-**
ROUND

65

"Go to hell" is no longer adequate
And because everything is reiterated
Just as our attempts create
For ONE, BEST, UNIQUE
Demented goat, disinherited mule
Go to Columbus

America changes together with us
And whatever way we wheel
America is at our heels

> *O bread, O horror*
> *Salt is flour*
> *And the taste of test*
> *Will never rest*

A stale taste in the mouth
In vain I flail about
These are someone else's daybreaks

A stale taste in the mouth
After wakes

Red thread
Of ice-cold water
And its white white route
With your mouth you can't stop doubt
It smiles and smiles
For miles and miles
The Indoamerican
The Americanindian
Wall around the heart

66

Christ walks on water

6 7

All go everywhere
At the end all stand
The end of ends
Could also be
Serene
It depends on how one
Understands
We must know how to sail
How to seek, how to see
And that we're of the sea and we shall be the sea
Is not true
We are only ordinary yellow dry land
And its brown precip-
Ice

God!
Faster!
And there thou goest
First

Flame of spheres
Break of spears
Nothing assists
Water is all
India isn't
India is

And since ice is of water
And since water is ice
Call forward back
Call back forward

Indiandering! Our golden
Indiandering! Long and heavy
Through darkness and rain, rain and darkness
Through salt and sea, sea salt
And all under the stars
Beautiful and dear, ours and beloved
As long as all lasts
As long as we last
On the way to the happy end
On the way to the land of lands
To come into force
Christaling Christofors

Ind and I
We race in a circle
We stare
At day at the hope
O cheerful, O joyful here
꞉~ You are and full
Is that then
India?

68

꞉~ In the Croatian original, these verses are palindromic: *U dan u nadu / O vedar o rad evo / Ti si i sit.*

69

Craggy morning
(NEW-MOSKVA)

The sky is high
The earth short
And pours vodka
Down our eye

How many those and one I
Call me NOHOW
India enters into all
Things and rapidly
Thins

70

The poet renounceth India
(Second fall beneath the picture)

The poet sat without, upon the deck. A sailor came unto him, saying to him, "Thou also hast been in India." But he denied before them all, saying, "I know not what thou sayest." While he was gone out into the captain's cabin, another sailor saw him, and said unto them that were there, "This fellow was also in India." And again he denied it with an oath, "I do not know that land." And after a while came unto him they that stood by, and said to the poet, "Surely thou art also hers; for thy song betrayeth thee." Then he began to curse and to swear, saying, "I know not the land." And immediately the wind blew. And the poet remembered the word of Columbus, which said unto him, "This night, before the wind blow, thou shalt thrice drown India in America." And he went out, and wept bitterly. Whereupon they arrived.

7 1

The discovery of America
(bitter step)

Under open sky
We are water's eye
We are pricked by
Water's freedom

There are darks
And here are we
India's horn
Gleams to us

72

:~ Never again the Land of the Grin
    Perhaps only the grin of the land

    Far from America
    Emerged the dark of a poem

    With the white marks of India

:~ Refers to the title of the operetta by Franz Lehar.

7 3

And the EAST gleams
In the name of the Same

The totem of the human band
From morning to darkness
Carries in all directions
The dust of pounded lands

East to the West is West
West to the East is East
Eggs break so easily

O how bitterly poor Columbus
Cried one morning on his newest
Circular cross

74

The world still had not bandaged the last American wound
But Columbus was already in the sign of a new "WHERE TO?"
And sailed

On the American wounds Columbus was horribly
Renewed. But not as a person
Rather as a poet

Between person and poet
Protrudes America

Grey
Height

                    Scream, O America, scream
       :~   *Of the crucified poet's crucified dream*

:~ Refers to the verses by Ivan Gundulić: "Proclaim, [O Morning Star,] proclaim / A
clear day proclaim!"

7 5

:~ *Congratulatory telegram*

(Clear next-to-last day. The poet mopes in the sun of America, raises the stuffed bird of a head and reads wearily, though proudly)

"The fraternal workers, peasants, youth and all the progressive forces of our society direct to you expressions of the sincerest support in connection with the action of 99 texts, hoping that you continue to be on top of the task, that you write about everything that explores (explodes) this Globe of ours. We, the young, are particularly proud of that part of your texts that express full consciousness of the values and responsibilities of the textual revolution that is being carried out at every step: in work collectives, in homes, in the fields. We greet most warmly the appearance of naked textors and textresses in the streets of our cities, as a contribution to the general jouissance and critical transcendence of remnants of the past. The logical succession in the development of the problem is a textual act in a public place, which is among us, and elsewhere too, still in swaddling clothes. We shall never, and we shall allow no one to, give a positive answer to the question "IS DARKNESS POSSIBLE?" Let nothing thwart you on the path to the great, bright, eternally rhapsodic

Selftext!"

IN VAIN...

Our ruler is We
And We is a collective river
Which pours into the sea
Of the Great Brutus of the Next Day

:~ An imitation of the genre of the "congratulatory telegram" sent to rulers in Communist regimes at times of celebration or crisis.

76

LATE IN THE PATRIARCHATE OF LIGHT

       Street of straight India
       Or years
            Of fear
                Of wear
                    And tear

Seas don't sea
But do see
Dawns don't dawn
But do down

In the overall race for might
From the sky falls
An enormous, wide
NIGHT OF THE WORD

       Endless shudder and iceberg of the wall
       Unmendable holes
       Arise in sight
       And there is no strophe
       For this catastrophe

77

Chris Topher crucified on T
It is very difficult to choose
It is very easy to lose

Skill of centuries:
To say to America—America
To India—India

But the mouth is
                    out
                        of use

78

MUSE OF REASON
(White voice)

> Let us desert the mouth
> It is empty
> In that desert is tested
> The final cloud
> Over the world

O WOE, REALITY
(Black voice)

> But what good is a cloud to us
> A neutral being of high sky
> We have our black **C**
> In Croatian it's written **K**
> And let our New Age
> Resound loudly to
> Bloom of the mushroom

> Loud music:
> *For fall*
> *For fall*
> *Of the wall*
> *For the same*
> *Bloc*
> *Of*
> *Black*

~ In the Croatian original, there are two palindromic verses: MUSE OF REASON
(*MUZA RAZUM*) and O WOE, REALITY (*AVAJ, JAVA*).

The Old and New Century
*(2 great **C**'s)*

79

CHRIST COLUMBUS
Cross circle
Upwards-downwards
Hither-thither
Crucifixion to crucifixion
Without resurrection
Discovery to discovery
Without covering
Paradise in heaven
Paradise on earth
Rivers and seas
Of blood

I see two **C**'s
As good old friends
And I cheer
With fear

INTO THE DARKNESS, INTO THE DARKNESS
INTO THE TOMB OF THE LAST JUDGMENT
CHRIST AND COLUMBUS
ARE AT THE END

> *And there's no sea around India*
> *And there's no eye to see the sea*
> *But margin and tempest*
> ∻ *But thrall for hurrah and gathering clothes*
> *Pray for a ray of truth*
> *Say a prayer for the globe*

∻ In the Croatian original, these verses are palindromic: *A rub i bura / A ruha zbor i rob za hura.*

88

Hell of lacquer
(For everyone)

(Several dozen brave young lads sing a song about the Great Day of Decay, which fortifies and strengthens, lifts up and throws down. And the last runway glitters.)

A thousand seas, and one crust　　　　　　**80**
Our flight is might
Our line is mine
And reddens our deal: real zeal
And reddens the enormous, spherical dust
And reddens the final
The fiercest pain—
Salt rain:
　　　　　　　Stark naked
　　　　　　　Home
　　　　　　　　　　Of the third
　　　　　　　　　　　　Rose
　　　　　　　　　　　　　　Rome

8 1

> ∿ *To sail or not to sail*
> *That is the question*
> *Without answer*

The wind is soul
And the soul of the wind
With the wind in us
Makes up a cross
A cross on the water
Is the mast
Souls of all lands
From the land in me
From me in us
From us into you
From you into thousands
And again conversely
Darkness! Darkness!
You arise
When wind breaks up the day
Into night
How simple it is!
We stud thrones with nails
We tramp through golden chambers
We place ourselves in blood
And blood from blood we rise
Into a dream
We fight our way through dense nocturnal madness
We drink from a daily Danish throat
The wind is our soul
And the soul of the wind blows for us
Listen
Footsteps...
The wind...
It reaches us

∿ Wordplay with motifs from Shakespeare's *Hamlet*.

Through towers
The spirit of night
Exhibits
Its new day
Spirit, don't go!
Wind, blow!
Only a moment more…
The world hinges on a moment
Is the wind wind?
Is the soul everything?
Or is it all the Same
Without Shame?

82

Thereafter a day of rest:
Seated the East
Easy as the West

The United Atoms:
EX-EX-EXPLOSION!
And?

The Demise of Light
Of a windswept sphere
A new era?
Yes!
MAMA NIGHT

Voice of India
(LISTEN! LISTEN!)

8 3   ILLY

        ADD

          OR

            ODD ESSAY

There is no third

(Explanation)   *That is the basic indea*
Of this Columbiad
Divine Europedy
Indiad & Odioussey

Third World War
Or Final Score

84

DISGRACE OF SPACE

The secondary still strikes
On the purple sand of Nothing
Dead are all the heroes
Large and small Geigers
Fervently measure the connection
Between single and double
Zeroes

— *When will be the Resurrection?*

85

Daybreak from outer space
Or horrible case

HUGE
OVAL
ROSY
RADIANT
INDIA'S
BALLOON
LIKE
EARTH

COLUMBUS'
ATOMIC
SHATTERED
EGG

And dread to breed
And give dread heed

The Happy End
That shall never come
For everything is endless
Just as the endless bursting of a circle
Into a thousand lost dots
Into all of us
In all directions
The atom tombs
Earth's hell in the sky's paradise
And earth's paradise in the sky's hell
The sky is ruddy
The all is bloody
For everything is truly round
Instead of India
America is found

The Age of Eternity is great
And step by step therefore
To nevermore
Nevershore

Golden pendulum

87

O mass mother
Through entirely new past light
The now fraternal step hurries into darkness
And darkness fraternally stretches
With five and more fingers
Above beloved multitudes
The wind pollenates with horror
The flower of all species
Warlike and conversely cities rise and die
The scent spreads
Of merry sex
Which crackles
From brief happiness
Amid a small cluster of staring
Mommies of the pages
Daddy-like sufferers
The wife of the final son
Gloom frightful and wet
Hangs herself out to dry
THE WORLD WILL BE WASHED
STRAW WANTS TO BE SPREAD
THE NEXT SHINING LAD
WISHES TO BE MET

88

Columbus in paradise

(At the gates of paradise the angel Columbus suddenly appears. A cheerful herd of old, battle-tested lads softly sings)

> *Indiot, indiot*
> Where have you been—nowhere
> What did you do—nothing
> And winter passed, now spring is already
> Your damned ship circumnavigates
> Worlds of summers
> Seas of tumors

∻   *Sweat and yet*

Metastases of steps or the question:

DO I GO?

89

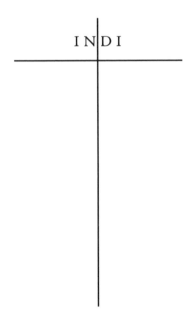

INDI

Great faith of Veronica
Everywhere already rages
The cancer of America

ERASE A PARADISE!

∻ In the Croatian original, this verse is palindromic: *kap i ipak.*

About the end of paradise
In the paradise of the end
(Cross, circle, and all of us)

90

The cross is crossed lines
The circle is a line around
And we're the dawn of exodus
Of a numberless number of lines
From the thousand and one points of the
NIGHT OF MIGHT

Once more
HOME DOWN

91

THE CROATIAN EGG
On the eve of the 500th anniversary of Columbus'
discovery of America

New nations are
Like stars
After the big bust
They originate
From dust

In a black zone
Croatia all alone
Spins around her core
And war

I.

This is no balcony
This is—the Balkans
These are no meadows
They are—Nevadas

Here night makes might
And a tomb is not a game
And there's no sight
To see and die of shame

This is not spring
No one ploughs this land
These words are said in vain
This is no century
These are no candles
These are our souls
Aflame

Worlds crash down
And candles melt
The butchered Balkans lie
Setting their paw
On Europe's throat
With a shudder and a cry

May 1991

II.

A little church—an apple
Shots—a shower
Biblical torture:
A bite out of the tower

Instead of harvest—curses
The gardener—slain
A hole in a school
A symbol of pain

And the Twelve?
Who and what are they?
The crust has burned
On the bread of Europe
Neither here nor there
The epitome of cynicism
Neither hide nor hair
And the warplanes fly

19 September 1991

III.

Poem in a bottle

From the legacy of Osip Mandelstam

Everything's mixed up, but I want to tell you:
Here the New Age ends in a wreck.
Everything's mixed up, and the words are fragile:
Baroque, Sezession, Osijek.

Everything's mixed up, but I need to tell you:
This is not a film shot, but sadder.
Everything's mixed up, and the words are horrible:
Arson, massacre, Zadar.

Everything's mixed up, but I have to tell you:
Throughout Croatia echoes a shriek.
Everything's mixed up, and the words are heavy:
Grenades, bombs, Dubrovnik.

Everything's mixed up, and I can tell you:
This Brotherhood's last Gift is war.
Everything is mixed up, and the words are sweet:
∾   Freedom, justice, Vukovar.

December 1991

∾ The cities destroyed by the Yugoslav army in 1991: Osijek and Vukovar in eastern
Croatia, Zadar and Dubrovnik in southern Croatia. The poem is a paraphrase of
the last stanza of Mandelstams poem *Dekabrist* (1917).

IV

Like the New World
A freedom is conquered
Not given when you beg

In order to be discovered
Croatia is broken
Like Columbus' egg

15 January 1992

92

I.

Europe '92

Five hundred years after
Such is the law of Columbus:
      Discovery
Of the United States of Europe

On the road to Indias
There is nothing to hinder us
Except America
Itself

II.

In the year 1492
Europe discovers America
In its own
Image

In the year 1992
Europe discovers itself
In the image of
America

This world, the same for everyone, was not created by anyone
      from among either gods or people
But it was, is now and ever shall be
America eternally alive
Which catches fire with measure
And with measure burns out

∼ Heraclitus

The question reads:

In the new Europe
In the new America
Who will be
The new Indians?

93

East of the West
West of the East
Every morning rises
A new America

And just when I thought that India was possible
That my house existed and a common European house
And just when I had sat down at the table to eat
On the television was the News
A tank came out of the grain
And said to me
"BON APPETIT!"

Thus I became
An Indian

And we wander towards Indias
And we wake up in Americas
We rub our eyes and cannot believe
That we have brought everything along with us
That we are in a society of old things, old alliances
At the same table, with the same pain
And that what we are drinking is not Indian tea
But an ordinary European despairing sea
Garnished with the eyes of Indians

94

> ∾ *Our beautiful homeland*

Our beautiful India
Which we shall never reach
For always along the way
We shall discover America
With wonder and a screech

Our beautiful India
Which lives in all things
Like be and not to be
Like darkness and like light
All Americas despite

∾ The first words of the Croatian national anthem.

9 5

In the heart of Europe
Or
∶∼ *East of history*

We stand
Between terror and hope
Pierced by an arrow
           Of the last India

And an evening falls
Which will never
Cease

AMERICAN PEACE

∶∼ This poem paraphrases Quasimodo's verses: "Each of us stands alone on the heart
of the Earth / Transfixed by a ray of sunlight / And evening soon falls."

96

What are we to India
And what is India to us
That we sail for her so
Bitterly

:~ *Indonamus et indonamibus*

97

Let us pray!

Our Columbus who art
In heaven and on earth
Give us this day
Our daily bread
Our daily
Dead

THE AMERICAN WAY OF LIFE
THE AMERICAN WAY OF DIE

98

*(One of a series
Of possible last wishes)*

Please, cut off my tongue
And throw it to the cats
The wind drives words
Towards the dead stars

99

America blows like the wind
And collapses like fool's gold justice
America falls like rain
Over our faces

And we shudder
From
America

COLUMBUS' TRIANGLE
Letter to the Ambassador of the
United States of America
to the
Republic of Croatia, Peter W. Galbraith

translated by Sibelan Forrester

Dear The Honorable Peter W. Galbraith,

You will surely ask yourself why I am writing this letter to you at all.
What can the problems of modern lyricism and contemporary Croatian
poetry have to do with you, the diplomatic representative of the most
powerful nation in the present-day world to little Croatia, which was
born in war and now with good will, though still uncertainly, takes steps
towards peace? What do you have to do with me and my poem?

I will say right away: very little and a great deal. In my poem, *American
Scream*, published in Croatian by the University Press in Zagreb (1981),
I played with the name of your country. More then, I took the name of
your country as the key word and idea of my poem. As the ambassador,
you are *today* the symbol of that name in the country where that poem
once came to be long ago. Allow me, then, to clarify how it was that the
poem *American Scream* came to be in the distant 1970s and 1980s, what
in my opinion that poem signified at the time it was written, and what
it seems to signify or could signify today, on the eve of the end of the
twentieth century.

You will forgive me, I hope, for the intimate tone, at least inasmuch as
that is a presupposition of any letter writing, including this kind of open
letter. If we can agree that style is the person, and literature a form of
autobiography, we need not be Freudians in order to seek many secrets
in childhood. Although I do not remember my father at all (for all traces
of him were lost after the end of the Second World War in May 1945),
I spent a very happy childhood in Slavonia, eastern Croatia, where I was
born. I was an only child and fatherless, and so my mother and the wider
family offered me more attention and love than was customary. Mama
and I waited for the first ten years for Papa to return, and when that did
not happen Mama began to live only so that one day we would go to
Zagreb and I would graduate from "the highest schools." And precisely in
that earliest childhood, while my experiences of space were limited to a
narrow triangle: Slavonski Brod (where papa was an officer in the Home
Guard and where he was seen for the last time), the village of Andrijevci

117

(where my grandmother and grandfather lived), and Borovo (where my mother worked after the war, in the greatest Socialist enterprise of former Yugoslavia, a rubber and shoe factory), three times, in three various surroundings, I met the name and image of your country. So even then, through those meetings and everything they could evoke in a child's imagination, your country impressed on my consciousness an undefined but powerful archetypal picture which long afterwards, though I have never been in your country, or perhaps for that very reason, would offer the key idea to my poem.

The first meeting with the word "America" occurred in the first grade of elementary school, in Borovo, when packages from UNRA arrived at the school. The teacher brought in large brown bags and said that the children without fathers should stand up. I stood up and received a package. I remember a hard yellow cheese and "Truman eggs" (the popular expression for the powdered eggs your country sent then as humanitarian aid). And just as I was reaching deeper into the bag in order to discover all its secrets, the teacher came back, and—the magic vanished. She took the package from my hands and said that it did not belong to me. I ran home in tears, and Mama comforted me with something that should have been an explanation, which I accepted, but which I actually did not understand. Namely, that my papa had not *perished* in the war, but rather—*vanished*, and that children of this sort could not get the wonderful American packages.

The other two meetings with the name of your country occurred a few years later, when Mama and I moved to my grandparents' in the village of Andrijevci, where a shop selling "Borovo" shoes had opened. My mother asked to be transferred so that we could more easily survive those hard postwar years (the country people, in spite of the victory of the working class, were still needed for socialism, and the country people needed rubber overshoes). No one, of course, wanted to go from the city to the village, naturally, so Mama got the transfer. My world became the movies, and all the movies in Andrijevci were American! They came on Saturday and Sunday, always new ones. *Gunfight on Silver Creek, High Noon, Gone with the Wind*...Of all the characters I got to like the Indians, and of the actors—all of them, without exception. We played Indians and wrote to the actors. The mailman had his hands full, bringing around postcards with the smiling faces of Audie Murphy, Tony Curtis, Elizabeth Taylor, Ava Gardner and tossed them, to the horror of our parents and neighbors, through the open windows, while on all sides of the dusty highway and in grassy courtyards our Indian arrows whizzed and incomprehensible nicknames echoed in the battle for the righteous Indian cause.

And finally, the third childhood meeting with America that was perhaps the most foreboding took place in the fifth grade of primary school, when we learned in geography that the world was round and had to make a plaster globe for our homework. Everyone wanted to make the most beautiful, the biggest and roundest globe in the world, but it wasn't easy at all; the plaster was hard to mix, and while we were adding the water it would already have hardened. We all got splattered by the white hardened mass, but we were extremely proud of our work. We learned that it was precisely because the world was round that the great Spanish seafarer Christopher Columbus (wanting to reach India from the west when the Ottomans forbade travel by the East) unwittingly discovered America. It all got mixed up for me. I was an excellent student, but now for the first time, something was unclear to me—especially with the directions in the world—and what was unclear to me seemed unjust and sad. I imagined the little Japanese on the other side of the world who had the same homework that we had and how for them, in Japan, America is actually in the east, while to us, in our village of Andrijevci, it was in the west. At the same time, I was horribly sorry for Columbus that he thought he had reached India, while he had really discovered America, and that America was named after Amerigo Vespucci, who only described the new continent, and not for him, Columbus, who discovered it. I got an "A" for my globe, like the whole class but that could not comfort me. It seemed to me that there was some irreparable flaw and injustice in the globe and its roundness. And when we went home that day with our As and our globes, the boys (among them was my future husband) started to play ball with the globes, and in that globe game one of the balls—one globe—hit our school friend on his big, blond head, which looked so much like a white plaster globe, and two days later he died. In the village they said that he had died of meningitis, but we knew that he had died from the globe. And so my memory of the globe, which was to blame for the unjust story of Columbus, was combined with something entirely horrible: tangible, real evil.

I can't say for sure when and why I took the name of your country for my poem's theme. I can only say that it was the basic idea of my poem.

The word "America" was never, at any moment or phase of writing, meant to be seen as the real country America represented by you in my country today. I was actually *playing* with the name of your country in the tradition of modern lyrical poetry: it was its fundamental idea, it is found in the title of the book and on all its pages. In my book "America" was always—a symbol, a metaphor. The poem, as I see it, was built as a linguistic and stylistic variation on the theme of one idea—the idea of modern European civilization as the history of the liberation of mankind and the realization of the Absolute (these are at first glance ponderous words, but I'll clarify them at once). Specifically, with the end of the Middle Ages (most often called "gloomy" in these lands in the time of Real Socialism, that is, in the era of my youth), in which the main field of culture was religion, people resettled God into themselves and the fundamental field of culture became History as the path of human liberation, that is "the end of alienation" and "the humanization of the person" (well-known expressions from the philosophy of my youth). Paradise (which religion and its cultural field, the Middle Ages, expected after the completion of earthly history in Heaven) in the Modern Ages by the laws of rationalism and enlightenment was supposed to be realized in human history on the Earth. In the person (let us remember Descartes' *Cogito, ergo sum*) and in human history (Hegel opined in his *Philosophy of the Spirit* history was finished and nothing important could be done or said anymore), such values as absolute freedom of the individual and the nation, absolute justice, equality, happiness, love, well-being, and finally an entirely classless society were supposed to be realized. In the name of those ideas and those ideals, the philosophers of the Modern Era built their theories, scientists discovered their inventions, poets sang their songs, and politicians fomented revolutions and conducted wars. Exhausted philosophical systems, outdated inventions, sung out songs, completed wars, and stifled revolutions were replaced by new ideas and new ideals in whose names there arose new philosophical systems, new inventions, new poems, new wars, and new revolutions. When it was proved that the posited ideals were not realized in those still newer systems, still newer inventions, and still newer songs and that their realization could not be achieved either by revolutions or by wars, that paradise on earth often resulted in purgatory or hell, everything would begin again from the beginning.

In that model of history there was an empty place, a black hole from which it always peered out anew, in which it completed its cycles and finally in our era came to an end. The name of that hole was *terror*. And that hole in modern history was the dark side of the idea of absolute freedom. When Hegel, speaking of revolutionary violence in the time of the French Revolution, poetically speculated on absolute freedom as "the night in which all cows are black," that was precisely the model for our Modern Era history, the two sides of its fundamental idea. Namely, the grandeur and misfortune of our modern history lay in the fact that the freedom bearer of that history was so elevated and so absolute that it could not be borne out in reality, and that for its realization some violence was always necessary, so that along with all the good intentions of the bearers of that freedom there were always some injustices and some disillusionments. That injustice and that disillusion, for their part, were the movers of a new cycle of that same history. Therefore, all Modern Era history was a history of polemical turns and inversions in philosophy, scholarship, and art (Kant topples Leibniz, Hegel topples Kant and the like, Classicism topples the Baroque, Romanticism topples Classicism, and so on), and in reality a history of wars and revolutions.

And precisely here, in Columbus' route to India and his unwitting discovery of something he wasn't looking for, of the new continent on which your country would arise, is the archetype of our Modern Era civilization and its modern history, just as Odysseus' travels to Ithaca were the model for the antique world and the civilization of the Ancient Era, and Golgotha for the Middle Ages. Thus it becomes clear why America, along with the other two concepts, Columbus and India, never meant, nor could ever mean, geographical and historical reality to me, why they were and remained symbols, metaphors.

As symbols and as metaphors these concepts were part of the archetypal triangle of Columbus—the Modern Era historical trinity which stands at the origin of modern European civilization. If it will not anger you, I would also like to show this Modern Era archetypal triangle graphically, so that the readers of this unusual letter can grasp my idea more easily and so that my playing with the name of your country will be simpler and more convincing:

121

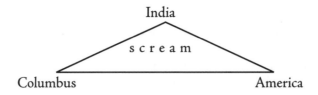

Columbus is the symbol of the man of the Modern Era, the individual who has replaced religion with history, who has resettled God inside himself, he is the symbolic *Father* of our modern history; India is the symbol of the Modern Era's idea of freedom, of all the utopian goals which modern humanity have set and most often have not realized or have let down altogether (*Spirit* of modern European history which in various forms is equal to the intentions and deeds of that person and that history); America is the symbol of reality which contradictorily and often unconsciously occurs on the path towards those goals and that idea (the *Child* of history so understood); and the "scream" is the symbol of violence and terror by which they have tried to realize the idea of freedom in reality, symbol of the birth pains of our modern history in which the father Columbus and the spirit of India always give birth to the child—America. Columbus is us, the individuals of the Modern Era, India is our dreams, ideas, and ideals about absolute freedom and happiness, America is the forms of life, institutions, and laws in which those dreams are realized or can be realized, and the "scream" (that is the manner in which those ideals are realized) the style of our modern European life and our modern history.

And so it went from Columbus' discovery of your land all the way up to the twentieth century. That archetypal triangle lived and directed our history only as long as any "scream" that would arise in that triangle had meaning. And the meaning existed only as long as the old cycle of the triangle would end in one "scream" and a new, supposedly "better" cycle of the triangle would begin, in which new individuals would create new ideas, new dreams, and on the path to those new ideas would discover a new, "better" reality, in order for everything to begin from the beginning on the endless path of liberation of humanity and human history.

A shift in this archetypal triangle came at that moment in modern history when two super-individuals appeared in our civilization, two dark Columbuses (in Nietzsche's words, *Übermensch*) who wanted finally to complete that archetypal image, that endless replacement of new individuals, new ideas, and new realities. These two "supermen" broke off the triangle (like Hegel, who did so in his philosophy), by coming forward with two super-ideas: *the idea of the best of all nations and the idea of the best of all worlds.*

As you surely guess, esteemed ambassador, those two last Columbuses of the Modern Era were named Hitler and Stalin, and their ideas were Nazism and Communism. And they, or rather their ideologies, asserted that those very ideas were the final ones, the best of all ideas; that on the way to that goal, to those two Indias, all means were permitted and all costs worth paying. Thus, the twentieth century became the century of super-violence. In the name of the first idea Hitler undertook the destruction of the Jews and the Second World War; in the name of the second idea there arose the first country of socialism, the Soviet Union, in which the "bourgeoisie" and the "dishonorable intelligentsia" were destroyed, and then the enormous Real Socialist empire, in which the Eastern and Central European peoples were enslaved (among them my country and my people). Thus, the twentieth century discovered two continents of evil: *Auschwitz* and the *Gulag Archipelago.* Your country fought against the first idea and its reality, defeating it in war. With the other idea and the other reality, after the great victory in the Second World War, it continued to coexist in a new world, divided "into two like a sliced orange" (as the Croatian poet Slavko Mihalić would say). And the very fact that the other idea remained alive, what is more, that in the divided world after the Second World War it even developed, spreading and confirming the space of its power, concealed the sudden aging of all the great utopian ideas, and by this of the very triangle of Columbus, without which these ideas do not exist.

And what happened then? Well, the aging of the last great idea of the Modern Era, Communism, and by the same token the aging of our archetypal triangle, continued unnoticed, and just as unnoticeably, after many more years and plenty of painful incidents (let's remember Yugoslavia in 1948, Hungary in 1956, Poland in the 1980s), that idea finally died. With the death of that last great idea, our archetypal Modern Era triangle died as well. This happened in the famous year 1968, when Russian tanks rolled into Prague and crushed the Prague Spring (on the eastern side of the divided world) and when, perhaps precisely because of that, the leftist student rebellion dispersed (on the western side of the same divided world). Everyone felt that something great happened that year, but then no one could yet say what. And we in Croatia experienced something similar in our own way two years later, in the crushing of the Croatian Spring in 1971–72. Then there came a time in which no new great idea could appear, no new utopian dream, for the ideas of fascism and communism had compromised all ideas of freedom and liberation, the soul of our modern history.

In your country this was first felt at the time of the war in Vietnam. The children of fathers who had been heroes in the struggle against Fascism in the Second World War no longer wished to be heroes, for there was no idea that could justify a war. It was, as Frederic Jameson noted, the world's first postmodern war. And afterwards, that sense that there was no longer *anything to wish, anything to dream*, and so then *anything to stand for*, seized the whole of society, the whole of Western civilization. Like a tower built of cards, all the great ideas collapsed: capital ruled instead of revolutions, sex instead of ideal love, advertisements and kitsch instead of high art, instant information from the electronic media instead of metaphysical insights from deep books. There were no longer any utopian dreams, no "Indias" which should be traveled to; there were no more great historical individuals, new "Columbuses," either. There remained only a naked civilizational reality, the metaphor of "America" and its monotonous "scream," which became a habit.

And precisely then, in that advanced point of the twentieth century, when Columbus' triangle was already dead but that was not yet known, my poetic idea arose. Like many others on the eastern half of the globe, I felt the death of Columbus' triangle in my own life, in my fate. And only two decades later, in 1989, when that real wall that had divided two worlds fell down, did everything become clear.

And so I see the structure and idea of my poem in the following way. In the title itself three suppositions interweave: the concept of "the American dream" in its everyday use, the title of Theodore Dreiser's *American Tragedy*, and the title of the poem *Howl* by Allen Ginsberg, translated into Croatian as *Urlik*. The theme of Columbus' triangle was varied on four basic levels:

1. On the level of contemporary American and Western civilization (motifs of abundance, jeans, television, Coca-Cola, speed, sex, and the like)

2. On the level of the Real Socialist empire and its ideology (clichés of thought and language in Communist society and Marxist philosophy)
3. On the level of intertextual patterns of the European and Croatian cultural traditions (quotations and paraphrases from Homer, the Bible, Ivan Gundulić, Tolstoy, and the like)
4. On the level of the apocalyptic collision of two worlds, the two sides of the world which defined Columbus' adventure: East and West (motifs of the "United Atoms," "mama-darkness," Columbus' broken egg, and the like).

Hugo Friedrich defined the modern lyric as a poetics of "empty transcendence." From that perspective, my poem *American Scream* was no longer a modern lyric, for there was no transcendence in it, not even an empty one. There was only the dead triangle of Columbus and its disconnected parts.

I would rather not tire you with a structural analysis of my own poem. The only thing I should still mention is the difference between the first Croatian edition and this American translation. Quantitatively, the difference is not great. Within the overall 100 texts (the introductory poem + 99), new texts have been inserted under the numbers 13, 18, 25, 28, 37, 91, 92, 93, 94, 95, and 97, and some motifs and verses now include notes. The amount of time which has passed between the publication of the original text and the translation has also led to a new way of reading the poem. In the 1980s, the poem was experienced as a linguistic game, but at the beginning of the new century, some of these games have assumed a deadly seriousness.

Symbols, as is well known, are those signs where there is a link between the sign and the reality signified, like the link between smoke and fire. In the first edition of *American Scream*, Columbus' whole triangle and the name of your country were for me the smoke which rose vaguely above the waters of modern European history. I played with that smoke. In this second edition, with the war that began in my country on the eve of Columbus' anniversary, I realized that there was fire behind that smoke and that this fire was great and horrible. I realized it was the fire in which Columbus' triangle had disappeared, and along with it, our modern history.

Your country, dear ambassador, as you of course know better than I, has long sat on the fence in the war on the Balkans. As the eldest child, and the inheritor of modern European history, it left Mother Europe to handle her final Modern Era scream herself. But when that did not happen, when the scream became so horrible that it could no longer be listened to, your country decided to take part in extinguishing it. The future image of our history and civilization will depend on how your country stands in this purely European matter, in this Balkan burial of Columbus' triangle. If your country becomes involved in this conflict so as to put an end to the balancing of blame for this destruction, for these contemporary conquistador-style campaigns, if your country feels compassion for the simple and intimate freedom of space, if it takes the side of the people and culture from whom that freedom was taken by force, our civilization will continue to develop according to the archetypal triangle of freedom. Columbus' triangle, which has died twice in the twentieth century, tortured by the dialectic of the "scream," would finally be buried, but ghostly history or emptiness would not appear on its grave, our history would not come to an end. Instead it would be renewed in a new freedom—the real and intimate freedom of space. And as every space has already existed forever, as every space is inhabited by some people, filled with some culture and surrounded by some nature, our history would no longer be the history of waiting for unknown worlds, a history of hope, as Ernst Bloch imagined it, but a "celebration of memory," joy for what exists, as Nietzsche said.

I cannot answer this and similar difficult questions in this letter. Nor are those answers to be found in my poem. I see the future of my poem, in so far as such a thing in literature, and especially in poetry, can be spoken of at all, precisely in its ability to provoke such questions. One thing, however, remains certain. If it is true that this war is deciding the fate of Columbus' triangle, and thereby of our civilization, your country, as the heir of that triangle, will become a part of our fate. What is more, it already is our fate. And that is noted in my poem.

In his pastoral play *Dubravka*, from which all the Dubravkas in Croatia received their name, including myself, the Croatian Baroque poet from Dubrovnik, Ivan Gundulić, sang a hymn to freedom in the seventeenth century. In his verses, the poet praised that same freedom which today, at the end of the twentieth century, is being trampled in this war. It was the freedom of specific people, a particular city and culture—the freedom of the Republic of Dubrovnik in the period of its flowering:

O lijepa, o draga, o slatka slobodo,
dar, u kom sva blaga višnji nam Bog je do,
    uzroče istini od naše sve slave,
uresu jedini od ove Dubrave. / ... /

Oh beautiful, oh dear, oh sweet freedom,
gift in which God on high gave us all blessings,
    you, cause of the truth from all our glory,
sole ornament of this Dubrava. / ... /

The grenades that fell on Dubrovnik at the end of the twentieth century
were grenades cast at that ancient freedom. And specifically because
I believe in such a clear and simple thing as Gundulić's freedom, I do
not doubt the freedom of my country. I do not doubt the will of your
country to stand up for that freedom. For after the death of Columbus'
triangle that properly addressed, small and fragile freedom is the
only India that is worth sailing for, the only America that is worth
discovering.

Respectfully,

Your Dubravka Oraić Tolić
In Zagreb, on the autumnal equinox 1994

PALINDROME APOCALYPSE

translated by Sibelan Forrester

1991
RIM I MIR
ILI
O N O

1991
ROME AND PEACE
OR
T H A T

I VISE SIVI
ISUSI

KRIK I

Nacrt europske civilizacije kao hoda po mukama (*Idu ljudi, I vise sivi / Isusi*) od biblijskih vremena (*Eno Noe*) do listopadske revolucije 1917. (*CAR U KURAC!*), kada počinje apokalipsa 20. stoljeća (*A l k a   p a k l a*)

AND GREY JESUSES
HANG

CRY I

A sketch of European civilization as it follows the Way of the Cross (*People go, And grey Jesuses / Hang*) from Biblical times (*The Eons of Noah*) to the October Revolution of 1917 (*TO HELL WITH THE TSAR!*), when the apocalypse of the twentieth century commences (D o o r b e l l   o f   H e l l)

133

Idu ljudi
Deru red
        — Molim? Molim?
        — Moli: silom!
A nada nenadana
O goni, nogo
Mobe nebom
Raž i žar
Eoni Noe...
        — Kamo, momak?
        — Čamu u mač!
I mač čami...
I sloga, a gol si
Tu ljut
Ilir...Ili?
Kanu junak
Tu ni ginut
Nebo-*oben*
        — Teret! Teret!
Mi—mači! I čamim
A Matija: RAJ I TAMA
I zob bozi
I boza zobi
Idu ljudi
Deru red
        — U kal tlaku!
Job i boj
Job u boj
I guraj k jarugi
Tup put
U jarku kraju
        — Uguraj u jarugu

People go
Rending order
          — If you please? Willingly?
          — Beg: by force!
And unexpected hope
Oh chase, leg
Gathering by sky
Rye and fire
The Eons of Noah…
          — Where to, lad?
          — Gloom into a sword!
And a sword to gloom…
And concord, but you're naked
Here angry
∽ An Illyrian…Or?
The hero avoided
Even dying here in peace
∽∽ Heaven-*oben*
          — Burden! Burden!
We are swords! And I languish
But Matthew: PARADISE AND DARKNESS
∾ And oats to boza
And boza to oats
People go
Rending order
          — Into the mud with corvée!
Job and battle
Job into battle
And push towards the ravine
A bluntly way
In the bright land
          — Push into the ravine

∽ Illyrian, ancient inhabitant of Balkan half island.

∽∽ *oben* (German), above.

∾ boza (Turkish), thick, sour drink made from wheat, corn, rice, and water.

Otac—OCAT! O...
I ta mati!
                    — Na tup stup!
          Put—sputan...
I tale džalati
E, te čete
U kraju, u jarku
Vir—kriv
O val, glavo
I val plavi
I val—mlavi
Idu ljudi
Deru red
                    — JA PUT SAM! Ma, stupaj...
                    — Istine nit si?
                    — Masa—ja sam!
I žuta luna, nula tuži
I siva luna, nula visi
Amo! Dosta!
At! Sodoma...
Idu ljudi
Urok oru
U roza zoru
Kaže težak:
                    — CAR U KURAC!
                    — TIRANI NA RIT!
O ti, žito
Uže vežu
I ruši, šuri
I tali lati

Mati! Hitam...
Modar radom
Harom orah
Napokon okopan
Vrt... — S T R V
On i dogovor?
               ROV, o godino!
               I vise sivi
                    Isusi

136

Father—VINEGAR! Oh...
And that mother!
                — Onto the blunt column!
        The way is fettered...
And the headsmen melt
Eh, those troops
Into the land, into the ditch
The whirlpool is guilty
Oh wave, head
And blue wave
And the wave batters
People go
Rending order
                — I AM THE WAY! Well, step lively...
                — Art thou not the thread of truth?
                — I am—the masses!
And the yellow moon, zero complains
And the grey moon, zero hangs
Hither! Enough!
Stallion! Sodom...
People go
They sow evil fate
Into a pink dawn
A peasant says:
                — TO HELL WITH THE TSAR!
                — TYRANTS ON THEIR ASSES!
Oh you, grain
They tie a rope
And it topples, blanches
And it melts blades

Mother! I rush...
Blue from work
I ploughed diligently
A finally hoed
Garden... — CARRION!
He and the agreement?
                PIT, oh year!
                And grey Jesuses
                Hang

Hej, psuj uspjeh!
Tovi život
I motrim: mir tomi
I zob bozi
I boza zobi

       A l k a   p a k l a

Hey, curse success!
Fatten up life
And I observe: peace wearies
And oats to boza
And boza to oats
            D o o r b e l l   o f   H e l l

DER RED
I
BRK SKRB

KRIK II

Vremenski niz apokalipse 20. stoljeća od Drugoga svjetskog rata do 80-ih godina: Hitler (Der *Red*) i Staljin (*Brk Skrb*), podjela svijeta na Jalti 1943. (*Tebi Tibet! / Nama Aman!*), stvaranje Istočnoga Socijalističkoga Carstva (*Suri ruj i juri Rus*) s Rezolucijom informbiroa 1948. (*I log—GOLI*), Mađarskom 1956. (*Rađa Mađar / Katar kratak*), raketnom krizom 1962. (*A Kuba? JABUKA!*), invazijom Čehoslovačke 1968. (*UGAR PRAGU!*) i slomom »Hrvatskoga proljeća« 1971. (*Hrvata vrh*); naftna kriza (*Niz nebo—benzin!*) i dolazak Homeinija na vlast (*Omamo, / i m a m i*); razotkrivanje ideje o najboljem od svih svjetova kao najvećem zlu (*UJEDI IDEJU!*) i izbor palindroma kao jezika apokalipse 20. stoljeća (*Hocke—rekoh / Ore pero*)

DER ORDER
AND
MOUSTACHE GUARDIAN

CRY II

Temporal series of the apocalypse of the twentieth century from the
Second World War to the1980s: Hitler (Der *Order*) and Stalin
(*Moustache Guardian*), the division of the world at Yalta in 1943 (*Tibet to
you! / Aman to us!*), the creation of the Eastern Socialist Empire (*The gray
red, and the Russian is rushing*) with the Resolution of the Informburo in
1948 (*And a lair is—NAKED*), Hungary in 1956 (*The Magyar gives birth
/ To a brief catarrh*), the rocket crisis of 1962 (*And Cuba? AN APPLE!*),
the invasion of Czechoslovakia in 1968 (*BLACK SMOKE TO PRA-
GUE!*), and the crushing of the "Croatian Spring" in 1971 (*The summit
of Croats*), the oil crisis (*Down the sky—gasoline!*), and Khomeini's rise to
power (*Oh stupor, / i m a m s*), the exposure of the idea of the best of all
worlds as the greatest evil (*BITE THE IDEA!*) and the choice of the
palindrome as the language of description for the apocalypse of the
twentieth century (*Hocke—I quoth / The pen ploughs*).

I bi
Rat na jantar
Rat unutar
Rat i hitar
Der Red
I
Brk Skrb
Ili
Laj »HEIL«
I
Gur Drug
Rim i mir
Mir i Rim
Romor! Gromor!
Romo—POMOR
Gol zar razlog?
Zar mraz?
Da l glad?
                    — Kamo, momak?
                    — NA ŽUR OBORUŽAN!
E, čudesan, zna se, Duce!
                 A b o r t u s   u t r o b a
Zar o poraz?
Rat unutar
O, ti ne bi, Benito
(Minu punim)
U jarku kraju
U grubu Burgu
Rez jak—*Kaiser!*
Tugo, *gut!*

And there was
War on amber
War within
War and swift-footed
∽   *Der* Order
And
Moustache Guardian
Or
∽∽   The bark "HEIL"
And
Shove Comrade
Rome and peace
Peace and Rome
Murmur! Thunder!
Roma—EXTINCTION
Really naked reason?
Really freezing?
And famine too?
                    — Whither, lad?
                    — TO A PARTY ARMED!
Eh, marvelous, it is known, Duce!
                A b o r t i o n   o f   w o m b s
Really about defeat?
War within
Oh, you wouldn't, Benito
(I fill a mortar shell)
In the bright land
∾   In a rude *Burg*
∾∾   The cut is strong—*Kaiser!*
∽∾   Sorrow, *gut!*

∽ *der*, definite masculine article in the German language.

∽∽ *Heil*, Nazi salutation.

∾ *der Burg* (German), fortress city.

∾∾ *der Kaiser* (German), Czar.

∽∾ *gut* (German), very well, OK.

143

Rat
    Log
        Oltar
            Ata! Ata!
At laje—JALTA
I val slavi:
      »DAMO KOMAD!«
        — Tebi Tibet!
        — Nama Aman!
        — Mi tuđe, međutim…
        — Ne daj Aden!
        — A, da…
        — VAŠ ŠAV!
        — Aha!
O nakano!
O kako?!
I
Ovom—ovo
Onom—ono
OK, jeko
I popi
I bobi
Il bol obli
      g o l o g
Kas i pisak:
      — NEOPISIV VISI POEN!
O zarazo
To ris sirot
Mori mirom
Tali Pilat
E, roza zore
Tih su ushit
Hada zadah
A Samson—os masa
Vi Dalila—div
I salva vlasi
It salva vlasti

144

War
    Lair
        Altar
            A horse! A horse!
A horse neighs—YALTA
And the wave celebrates:
      "WE GIVE A PIECE!"
        — Tibet to you!
        — Aman to us!
        — We're taking someone else's, however...
        — Don't give Aden!
        — Ah, yes...
        — YOUR STITCH!
        — Aha!
Oh intention!
Oh how?!
And
To this one—this
To that one—that
OK, echo
And the priests
And the beans
And a round pain
        of the naked one
Gallop and squeak:
        — AN INDESCRIBABLE POINT HANGS!
Oh infection
That lynx wretched
Slaughter by peace
Pilate melts
Eh, pink dawns
Quiet are rapture
Stench of Hades
And Samson—axis of the masses
You Delilah—giant
And salutes of locks
   It salutes of power

~ *it* (Latin), third person present from the verb *ire*: to go.

Idi!
Ume, čemu?
I rat stari
Mori širom
Umuj, umu
Modar gradom
Modar kradom
Suko okus
Rat star
Okolo loko

                — MIR KOMUNIZMU!
                        (Um zinu. Mokrim...)
Suri ruj i juri Rus
Brk Skrb! Brk Skrb!
On eno
        Ide!
            »JEDI
                SVOJ OVS!«
I Brk skrbi

            O JUGO! O GUJO!
Dah nade—jedan Had
Rim i mir
Mir i Rim
I romor romori
I Roma—mori
Ini sini
I?
            Piso Josip
I?
            Sipo opis
I?
            Sipo popis
I log—G O L I ...

Go!
Mind, for what?
And war ages
Slaughters all over
Ponder, mind
Blue through the city
Blue by stealth
Twisted taste
Old war
Carouse around
              — PEACE TO COMMUNISM
                 (Mind gaped. I urinate…)
The gray red, and the Russian is rushing
Moustache guardian! Moustache guardian!
Look there he
        Is coming!
           "EAT
                YOUR OWN OATS!"
And the Moustache of Guardianship
              OH YUGO! OH SERPENT!
Breath of hope—one Hades
Rome and peace
Peace and Rome
And murmur murmurs
And Roma—slaughters
Other sons
And?
        Josef wrote
And?
        Scattered description
And?
        Scattered a list
And a lair—N A K E D …

:~ "Oh Jugo," vocative of "Juga," slang term for Tito's Yugoslavia.

:~:~ Josef, refers to the first names of Stalin (Josif Visarionovič) and Tito (Josip Broz).

~: "Naked Island" ("Goli otok") was a Yugoslav concentration camp in the 1950s and 1960s.

147

Nisi sin
Ni mamin
Ni tatin
I srsi, srsi
A nemir imena?
NA ME NEMAN!
Mi—dim, vi—div!
SAN! A danas?
O goni, nogo
Kala lak i laka kal
Uhu!
Umre nježni inženjer mu...
Melem!
Ali, mila
Usud usu
Paku kap
Tapa šapat
Mori pirom
A l a z a l a
— U-u-u-u-u-u-u
Ruska tema: metak sur
Rido dodir
Rat star
Nov On
BRK SKRB
On žali lažno
On vara, naravno
On voli—lovno
Oni ino
A
On redom moderno
Široko koriš
Široko pokoriš
»Mogu rugom!
Mogu tugom!«
Misa...
P a s i m...
»SAVEZ UZE VAS!«
I nakani
»Nema—i amen!«

148

You aren't a son
Neither mama's
Nor papa's
And shudderings, shudderings
While the unease of a name?
                    A MONSTER ASSAULTS ME!
We are smoke, you are giants!
A DREAM! And today?
Oh chase, leg
Lacquer of slime and slime of lacquer
Oho!
His tender engineer died...
                    Balm!
But, my dear
Fate poured in
A terrible drop
A whisper tiptoes
Slaughters with a wedding-feast
D r a g o n   o f   e v i l
                    — U-u-u-u-u-u-gh
A Russian theme: a gray bullet
Touch sobbed
War old
New He
                    MOUSTACHE GUARDIAN
He pities falsely
He deceives, of course
He loves—huntingly
They take their way
And
He makes his modern way
You blame broadly
You subjugate broadly
"I can by mockery!
I can by sorrow!"
A mass...
                    Up t h e i r s...
          "THE UNION TOOK YOU OVER!"
And intended
"There's nothing and amen!"

149

Nemilo limen
I
Tako okat
At šepa: PEŠTA
Rađa Mađar
Katar kratak
Dug ud
A Kuba? JABUKA!
Inat...Stani!
Rim šanu: "Naš mir!"
Ures!
            — Seru!
U Rimu—UMIRU!
Varav Rim!
       I mir—varav...
Suko okus
Suko pokus
Vidi div
Div, a David
       Golijat taji log
Da! Nato t a n a d ...
Sueza Zeus
           — AMANETOM OTE NAMA!

A humana muha?
O humana muho!
Kazo mozak
      »On daje jadno!«
Časak...KASAČ!
Tako okat
Nov on
Voli lov
      »O mi želimo...«
          Mi—ležimo!
Gol log
Jačo očaj
»U jami imaju
        jači čaj!«
Ure beru
Noć! On!

Ruthlessly tin
And
So big-eyed
The horse limps: BUDAPEST...
The Magyar gives birth
To a brief catarrh
Long joint
And Cuba? AN APPLE!
Spite...Stop!
Rome whispered: "Our peace!"
Decoration!
                 — They are shitting!
In Rome—THEY ARE DYING!
Rome is deceitful!
         And peace—is deceitful...
Twisted taste
Twisted test
The giant sees
The giant, and David
         Goliath conceals the lair
Yes! Thereupon b u l l e t s ...
Zeus of the Suez
              — THEY STOLE IT FROM US
                  WITH A PLEDGE!
And the humane fly?
Oh humane fly!
The brain said
      "He's stingy!"
A moment...A HORSEMAN!
So big-eyed
And new
Loves hunting
      "Oh we desire..."
                We—lie down!
Naked lair
Strengthened despair
"In the pit they have
         stronger tea!"
Hours fly by...
Night! He!

151

BRK SKRB!
                    — UGAR PRAGU!
Hitar vratih
Rada dar
Nade dan
A mama?
A tata?
DAJ JAD!
Ti—budi Vi! I vid ubit...
Ti—za gazit!
O, mi zagazimo...
Suri ruj i juri Rus
Ah, opet epoha
I?
                    Model ledom!
I?
                    More Sibirom. Ori biserom...
Rat star
Nov On
I voli i lovi
I lovi i voli
              K o   p s a !
                              MAS-POK...
E, dani nade
I mladi Dalmi
Hrvata vrh
Dol. Plod
              Siv
                    Vis
NATO GETO TEGOTAN
O mrka krmo
I
Čara harač
Umuj, umu
              Niz nebo—benzin!
Zalud ulaz
Para Arap
Napaja Japan
A Tula luta
                    KULUK?

MOUSTACHE GUARDIAN!
— BLACK SMOKE TO PRAGUE!
I returned quickly
Gift of work
Day of hope
And mama?
And papa?
GIVE GRIEF!
Thou—be you! And vision is killed…
Thou—to be trampled!
Oh, we started to trample…
The grey red, and the Russian is rushing
Ah, again an epoch
And?
A model by ice!
And?
They kill with Siberia. Harvesting pearls…
War old
New He
Both loves and hunts
And hunts and loves
L i k e   a   d o g !
MASS-MOVE…
Eh, days of hope
And young Dalmates
The summit of Croats
Valley. Fruit
Gray
High
THEN A DIFFICULT GHETTO
O stern stern
And
A witchly tribute
Reason, have a mind
Down the sky—gasoline!
In vain the entry
An Arab rips
Japan supplies
And Tula strays
LABOR?

153

Oho?!
Resi biser
Talir krilat
                    Oseka, keso!
Idu ljudi
Mole čelom
O maso, samo…
Omamo,
          i m a m i
Puk: s nabora čaroban skup
I rat stari
I duh hudi
E, nema mene
A bez zeba
I srsi, srsi
— SAVAK? A Vas?
— Halo?!
          (Tajac)
                    AJATOLAH:
                              — Idu?
                                        — Smrt!
                                                  (Strm sudi)

I rado podari
Kore rok
RAZLOG? Gol zar…
I tupi puti
Top! Tap!
Pot! Pat!
On? Ja?
                    TELAD! Ubiti budale tajno!
I nevini, veni!
I livade ne da vili
          Tada zadat?!
Tada—Sadat!
          A papa?
          A papa?
U gomili—mogu!

154

Well?!
A bead bedecks
A winged thaler
                    Low tide, purse!
People go
Pray with the forehead
Oh masses, only...
Oh stupor,
                    i m a m s
A mob: from the fold a magical gathering
And the old war
And the evil spirit
Eh, there is no me
And without shivering
And shudderings, shudderings
∴   — SAVAK? And You?
       — Hello?!
                    (A silence)
                              AYATOLLAH:
                                        — Are they coming?
                                             — Death!
                                                  (Judges cruelly)

Takes pleasure in creating
The fate of the world
Does this make SENSE? Are we really naked...
And ways dense
Hip! Hop!
Sweat! Duck!
He? I?
                    CALVES! To kill fools secretly!
And the innocent one, wither!
And the meadows aren't given to the fairies
          Should we cut them?
Then—Sadat!
          And the pope?
          And the pope?
In a throng I can!

∴ SAVAK, abbreviation for Iranian secret police.

155

Noga vagon
Uđe među
Mati, pitam:
        Ide neki Kennedy?
A tama kamata?
Suri ruj i juri Rus…
      UJEDI IDEJU!
I Bog u Gobi
I Brk skrbi
I vise sivi
Isusi
Oganj, ago
      Ugar tragu!
      Ugar pragu

                          m o m
Kazuj uzak
Bobu bob
A
Popu pop
Rovo govor
Hocke, rekoh
Dere nered
Dere red
Niče čin
      Eseji! Vani mrak karmina vije se
      Niti Tin
      Riše šir
      O mi ljubimo!
      O mi buljimo!
             (Upužu u župu)
I ne ču učeni
I ne ču tučeni
I ne ču mučeni

The train full of legs
Went in between
Mother, I ask:
      Is some Kennedy coming?
And the darkness of interest?
The gray red, and the Russian is rushing...
      BITE THE IDEA!
Both God in the Gobi
And the Moustache of Guardianship
And grey Jesuses
Hang
Fire, oh lord
          Black smoke to the trace!
          Black smoke to the threshold of my
               h o m e

Say it easy
A bean's a bean
And
~   A priest's a priest
Trench tells the truth
~:~ Hocke, I quoth
Rends disorder
Rends order
The deed sprouts up
      Essays! Outside the darkness of carmine flutters
~:   Nor Tin
      Draws broad
      Oh we kiss!
      Oh we miss!
          (They crawled into the parish)
And the learned didn't hear
And the beaten didn't hear
And the tortured didn't hear

~ In Croatian phraseology: to call a spade a spade.

~:~ Gustav René Hocke, author of *Mannerism in Literature* (*Manierismus in der Literatur*, 1959).

~: Augustin (Tin) Ujević, modern Croatian poet (1891–1955).

157

Ne ču! Od nedoučen
Ne ču! Oko sivo! Visokoučen...
Hocke—rekoh
Ore pero
Okati, okati
DIV—VID
Itako, Itako
O krik!
Idi
Arkom
Mokra
Kirko

Didn't hear! He went away unlearned
Didn't hear! Gray eye! Highly taught…
       Hocke—I quoth
       The pen ploughs
       Big-eyed, big-eyed
       A GIANT—A SIGHT
            Ithaca, Ithaca
                Oh cry!
                    Go
                      By ark
                          Wet
                            Circe

NACRT OTRCAN

KRIK III

Poljska 80-ih

WORN OUTLINE

CRY III

Poland in the 1980s

Otud uto
Kaljo Poljak
Rob. Zbor
Mir! O zorim...

                Mjesec. E...Sejm...
                A papa?
                A papa?
U Rimu je! Ej, umiru
Zar mraz?
Da l glad?
Tema: N A M E T
Ljeti lom. Molitelj
I jarma raj i jaram raji
                Jaram—umaraj!
I rob zbori
I rob ori
Oko si visoko
Oko budi duboko
I budi dub i
Bure rub
Muk
        Um
Odu čini...Čudo!
Tužbo, rob žut!
A sela, Walesa?
I dulji ljudi?
              GOL ULOG
E, neće, ne
Tavorit i rovat
Narod oran
Reče večer:
            Ovo novo?

O meteže! Teže, temo
            Novo: » *Von!*«
ANARHO–HRANA?

From here meanwhile
The Pole tainted
Slave. Meeting
Peace! Oh I ripen…
                    A month! Eh…Sejm…
                    And the pope?
                    And the pope?
He's in Rome! Eh, they're dying
Really a freeze?
And famine?
The theme: T O L L
In summer breaking. The supplicant
Both paradise of bondage and bondage to people
                    Bondage—tire!
And the slave speaks
And the slave resounds
Your eye is high
Eye be deep
And be an oak and
The edge of a storm
Stillness
            Mind
Witchery has departed…A miracle!
Grievance, a yellow slave!
And the villages, Walesa?
And longer people?
                    NAKED STAKE
Eh, it won't, no
Eke out a living and root up
The vital people
The evening spake:
                    Is this new?

Oh chaos! Harder, oh theme
                    The new: "Von!"
ANARCHO–FEED?

∿ "Von!," in Russian, "Get out of here!".

Da! Pa... Zapad!
Ne žal blažen
Tako? Nakot si... Istoka nokat!
I ti bi biti?
I ti u niz! Zinu i ti!
Da, jad...

O k a j j a k o
N a z o r g r o z a n !

Osamo, maso!
I tamo, mati!

— MELJI!

(Demarš rame diljem)
Sok olova đavolokos

ENO TOP

(Potone)
Dana tanad
A tane: melem »elemenata«
Nemir

K r i m e n !

Varav
Mit

(ušutim)

Yes! Well…The West!
Not a blessed beach
So? You're a brood…Fingernail of the East!
And you'd like to be?
And you into a row! You also yawned!
Yes, distress…

                  A t o n e   s t r o n g l y
            F o r   t h e   a t r o c i o u s   n o t i o n !

Oh loneliness, oh Mass!
And Mother darkness!
        — GRIND!
                (Demarche rocks the Bloc)
Devil-haired juice of lead
        THERE A CANNON
              (It drowned)
Bullets of days
And the bullet: balm of "the elements"
Unease
        C r i m e n !
     Deceitful
     Myth
           (I fall silent)

UVOD U UDOVU
ILI
ATI IDU, JUDITA

KRIK IV

Atomska apokalipsa: Černobil 1986

INTRODUCTION TO A WIDOW
OR
HORSES ARE COMING, JUDITH

CRY IV

Atomic apocalypse: Chernobyl in 1986

Hita kas sakatih
Opaka kapo
I bos u sobi
Buke kub
Te pamtimo mit »Muppet«
Učini! Niču!
I rok ori
I romor romori
Atom nas u san mota
               Je li lago Galilei?
Idu ljudi
Na rub buran
Tema: PAMET
O, ne!
Eno!
           Opor veo, Evropo!
I
U dim idu
Sol i los
Ris i sir
Riža. Žir
A jaja?
A krave?
         VARKA
O, ni vino…
Aroma mora
I vsë. Svi…
I Bog u Gobi
Uveo Evu
Mada Adam
I želi i leži
I ljubi i bulji
Avet Eva
Ote ljeto
Ave, Eva
Mota atom
I vi živi?
Napola galopan

168

A trot of cripples throws
Oh malignant cap
And barefoot in a room
A cube of noise
And we recall the myths of "Muppet"
Do it! They sprout up!
And a deadline resounds
And a murmur murmurs
The atom reels us into sleep
                    Did Galileo lie?
People go
To the stormy edge
Theme: REASON
Oh, no!
There it is!
            A crude veil, oh Europe!
And
They go into the smoke
Salt and reindeer
Lynx and cheese
Rice. Acorn
And eggs?
And cows?
            ILLUSION
Oh, not even wine...
Aroma of the sea
∾   And *vsyo*, Everyone...
And God in the Gobi
Led Eve in
Even though Adam
Both desires and lies
And kisses and stares
The ghost Eve
Kidnapped summer
Ave, Eve
The atom reels
You too are alive?
Galloped by halves

∾ *Vsyo*, (Russian), everything.

O kas ako
O ako...Kao
Milo molim
Nade dan
Zalud ulaz
I rog gori
I rok skori
I vode redovi
Na žur ružan
Ili, mili
U golu ulogu
Mati—ritam

          MATIRA ARITAM!

I mi
       Ovo
I vi
       Ono
Orati, gitaro
Morati—gitarom
Potop?
Topot?
O, mi vrvimo
I dulji ljudi
Mole jelom
Rada dar

         A papa?
         A papa?

Kara rak
Tare rat
Rim—put! Tup—mir...
O gorda drogo

         Ovom ovo
         Onom ono

Ljulja ljulj
Kuha huk
Ore pero

Oh trot if
Oh if…As
Dearly please
Day of hope
Vain entry
And the horn burns
And the deadline speeds up
And ranks lead
To an ugly party
Or my dear
Into a naked role
Mother—rhythm!
        CHECKMATE ARRHYTHMIA!
And we
    This
And you
    That
To plough, oh guitar
To have to—with a guitar
A deluge?
A trampling?
Oh, we swarm
And longer people
Beg with food
The gift of work
       And the pope?
       And the pope?
Cancer castigates
War erases
Rome—way! Peace loses the day…
Oh proud drug
      This to this
      That to that
The cockle weed swings
Cooks the roar
The pen ploughs

OD—DO
Omiš ori: »Hirošimo«?
Skok u koks?
Pokop!?
Ni Babin
                   kuk!?
Mi, tuđe, međutim...
                M o l i   l o m !
I, Ružo, požuri
I šuga zaguši...
Hod: »Oh!«
Had, ah...
Rado bodar
Rado—odar!
A ta jata...
Ali, mila
Tame mat
Kamen. Kiše. Šikne
                         M A K
Idu sudi
O, već evo
        Uvod u udovu!
I žeži!
I žeži!
        I vise sivi
        Isusi
Izmet u Temzi
Cezij i zec
        Ima! A mi?
I mi...
I vi...
Evo zove
MUZA RAZUM

FROM—TO

:~ Omiš resounds: "Hiroshima?"
Suddenly coal and ashes?
Burial!?
Not even Babin

:~:~   Kuk!?
We don't want someone else's, however…
         P r a y   f o r   r u p t u r e !
And, Rose, hurry up
And the scab suffocates…
Gait: "Oh!"
Hades, ah…
Gladly clear
Gladly—a bier!
And those flocks of birds…
But, my dear
Checkmate of darkness
Stone. Rain. There suddenly gushed
         P O P P Y
The Day of Judgment is commencing
Oh, this already
     Introduction into the widow!
And burn it!
And burn it!
     And gray Jesuses
     Hang
Scum in the Thames
Even a rabbit
     Is radioactive! And we?
Yes, we are…
And you too…
Here calls
THE MUSE OF REASON

:~ Omiš, a Croatian town on the Adriatic coast.

:~:~ Babin Kuk, a suburb of Dubrovnik.

173

Ali, mila
Mazi mi se pesimizam
Reve never
I časak…

        K a s a č i !
        Nas—

            Nema!

                Amen!

                    San…

Onda, radno
Onda—na dno!

      O lapor! Piši—propalo!

But, my dear
Pessimism cuddles up to me
Never storms
And one moment...
                   T r o t t e r s !
                   We—
                           don't exist!
                                    Amen!
                                    A dream...

Then—get to work!
Then—hit the dirt!

                 Oh marl! Right as nails—it failed!

JARKI KRAJ

KRIK V

Hrvatska 1991: biblijska razaranja (*O Romo—Gomoro*), bombardiranje Zagreba (*Ilica? / Bacili???*); završni prizori apokalipse

BRIGHT END

CRY V

Croatia in 1991: Biblical devastation (*Oh Roma-Gomorrah*), the bombardment of Zagreb (*Ilica? / They threw it???*); final scenes of the apocalypse

Et Arba
Et urbe
E, Brute
A, brate…
Ma razaraj! I ja razaram
                    A tip pita:
                    — POKUS?
                                        U k o p?!
                    — Da, SAD!
                                        Utoli, pilotu!
                    I Lot—utoli…
                    Gar? Tane? Neee!
                                NATRAG
                    — UDAR GRADU!
                    O Romo—Gomoro
                    At susta
          Radar
                         I
                    On vidi divno:
          TRG—RT!
                    A ja
                    I ti
                    I mi
                    I vi
                    (Jako):
                                        — KAAAJ?
          Ilica?
                              Bacili???
          A? Da–da…

Et Arba

∼ *Et urbe*

Eh, Brutus…

Ah, brother…

So destroy! I too destroy

And some guy asks:

— A TEST?

B u r i a l?!

— Yes, N O W!

Quench, oh pilot!

Lot too—quenched…

Soot? Bullet? Nooo!

BACKWARDS

— An ATTACK ON THE CITY!

Oh Roma—Gomorrah

The horse is tired

The radar

And

He sees wonderfully:

THE SQUARE—A PIER

While I

And you

And we

And you all

(Strongly):

— WHAAAT?

∼∼ Ilica?

They threw it???

Ah? Yes-yes…

∼ *Arba* (Latin), a Croatian island, Rab; *Et urbe* (Latin), part of the phrase: *orbi et urbi*, to announce news or messages to the city and entire world.

∼∼ Ilica, a main street in Zagreb.

O   N   O

I to idioti
A T O M   S M O T A
Nama aman…
Ata! Ata!
Romar—mramor
Oganj, ago!
Kisik! Kisik!
Nama—zaman
Teleks: »SKELET!«
(Roza razor…)
K A L
    B O L
       O B L A K

Idi!
    Vidi!

T   H   A   T

And it's idiots
T H E   A T O M   R E E L S

Please, save...
A horse A horse!
Pilgrim—marble
Fire, oh lord!
Oxygen! Oxygen!
To us—in vain
The telex: "A SKELETON!"
(Pink destruction...)
S L I M E
    P A I N
        A   C L O U D

       G o!
          S e e!

181

The bombing of the Presidential Residence: Zagreb, 7 October 1991.
Photo: Hrvoje Knez. Zagreb City Museum

THE STORY OF
THE PALINDROME

translated by William E. Yuill

The First Part of the Story
or the
Croatian Spring of 1967–71

The story begins on a specific day, month, and year: 17 March 1967. On that day in Zagreb, the capital of the Republic of Croatia in former Yugoslavia, the *Declaration on the name and the position of the Croatian literary language* was published and condemned. The Declaration opposed the idea of a uniform Yugoslav language, cloaked under titles such as the Serbian or Croatian language, Croatian or Serbian, Serbocroatian, or Croato-Serbian (with or without a hyphen). The basic argument of the Declaration was that every nation had the right to call its language by its national or popular name and to develop it in keeping with its traditions. An unprecedented hue and cry was raised in public opinion and the media—the signatories of the Declaration were called upon to withdraw their signatures, and working people were told to condemn both its text and the signatories.

In many of its features, the story conforms to the model of a novel by Milan Kundera, *The Joke*. The theme of the story was the same: an utterly trivial, private criticism of Utopia and the heroes who dared oppose it. In Kundera's *The Joke*, the principal character ridiculed the Communist Party, which was sufficient to change the course of his life. In our "joke," the main protagonists were a pair of students (one male and one female), and the part of Utopia was played by the idea and practice of a common Serbocroatian or Croatoserbian language.

When the hue and cry was raised over the Declaration, the female character realized that behind the grotesque coining of national names for the Croatian and Serbian languages there lay a utopian, Orwellian Newspeak. The male character was working at that time as an intern at some school or other, where he happened to speak in favor of the Declaration in a private conversation. Enraged Utopia had found its anonymous victim. The shameless student was expelled from the school, and it was decided at a meeting of the Party organization that an investigation against him should commence.

The model of Kundera's novel now changed. Our two characters succeeded in taking refuge in Vienna after passing through the refugee camp in Traiskirchen and registered for classes at the University of Vienna. They lived in the Rögergasse, near the Friedrichsbrücke, and worked at various jobs.

From that hallowed year of 1968, certain improprieties on the part of the authorities of the University of Vienna have remained in the memory of our characters, along with a vivid image of Russian tanks in Prague on the TV screen in the student cafeteria in the Führiggasse. All the impressions of those years have been eradicated by the memory of a small room and a large TV screen beside the bar, with tanks in the foreground. The Prague Spring was crushed, but its virus had already infected Croatia, which was not that far away. Institutions and individuals, signatories of the Declaration, once more became active. And our two nameless refugees in Vienna also stirred into life. In the spring of 1970, a "spring" in the literal as well as the spiritual sense of the word, our two characters returned home. Elements of the Kunderan model began to manifest themselves again. Both of them were deprived of their passports for eighteen years. This was normal—the minimum penalty for actual or chance participants in the "spring."

It was not until twenty years later that the female character found herself once again in Vienna—in the spring of 1990, with a group of students from Zagreb who had come at the invitation of the Russian Department at the University. She was plagued by nostalgia and went in search of the house in Rögergasse 27, apartment 29. The numbers of the apartments skipped from 28 to 30; there was no 29 in Rögergasse 27. Someone had bricked it up. Nor was there any longer a student cafeteria in the Führiggasse.

The Second Part of the Story, or Croatian Literary Postmodernism

With the collapse of the Left in Western Europe and the Prague Spring in 1968, modern culture came to an end. That year two grand Utopian ideas expired: the idea of the best of all possible worlds (Communism) and the idea of permanent revolution (Neo-Marxism). In Croatian culture, postmodernism began with the collapse of the Croatian Spring of 1971. In that year a Balkan utopian synthesis also died: Yugoslavia + Communism = Titoism. Looking back today, when there is no longer a "Real Socialist empire", in the name of which the Prague Spring was eradicated, nor the power that implemented the eradication, the Soviet Union, when Tito's Yugoslavia has disintegrated in death and bloodshed, two basic paradigms in the cultural history of the twentieth century emerge: Utopia and Nostalgia.

The basic feature of Utopian thought and expression is an attempt to eliminate all opposites and the creation of an ABSOLUTE. The central Utopian idea of modern and avant-garde art was a belief in the demolition of the "institution" of traditional mimetic art based on opposition between the sign and the object, art and life, and the creation of a totally new art, and hence of a new civilization in which there would be neither these nor any other differences. In the name of the grand Utopian idea, modern and avant-garde artists, on the one hand, denied the category of the signified and absolutized the structure of the signifier to the point where they denied the logical structure of a text and creation ex nihilo (in painting, for instance, Malević's Black Square on a White Background; in poetry, the transrational "zaumnaja" poetry of the Russian Futurists and the global Dadaists). On the other hand, they equated the sign and the object (pears and apples cut from a newspaper and pasted on to a collage by Picasso, iconic signs in Döblin's Berlin Alexanderplatz, instead of a verbal description of the objects to which they refer). In their desire to create an absolute art beyond all semiotic opposites, the avant-garde and modern artists either rejected any type of structure (mechanically combined newspaper cuttings of Tristan Tzare), or created absolute shapes (collages, ready-made, various kinds of Gesamtkunstwerk). The modernistic and avant-garde faith was sustained by an expressly monologic consciousness—a huge "I" that aggressively imposed its Utopian will on the reader.

Modern and avant-garde art was alive as long as the Utopian faith in the power of art to demolish tradition and create and absolutely new art and civilization was alive. Great artistic works of the twentieth century issued from this Utopian faith, but the Utopian aims themselves were not achieved. Traditional art was not demolished, and the new art was not as absolutely new as its creators had anticipated and expected. Malević's Partial Eclipse (in which a reproduction of the *Mona Lisa* had been crossed out with a brush-stroke) or Duchamp's *Mona Lisa* with

189

a moustache, belong just as much to the products of European art as Leonardo's masterpiece, which they were attempting to demolish.

In the '70s, postmodern artists no longer wished to negate the logical structure of a text nor to create vague and unmanageable structures, as their modern and avant-garde predecessors had done. The main principle of postmodern art became the principle of intertextuality and quotation. Art and the world were understood as a library (for instance, in Umberto Eco's novel, *The Name of the Rose*) or as a museum (the Russian writer Andrej Bitov called his novel Pushkin's House a "novel-museum"). A desire for the revival of the known, or the use of popular ideas, was matched by the renewal of traditional and simple forms (Eco's novel, *The Name of the Rose*, is a detective novel based on a medieval theme; Magris' novel, *The Danube*, is a travelogue on the subject of Central European culture).

The consciousness that sustained postmodern structures was a modest dialogue "I" that attempted to get as close as possible to its interlocutor. Modernistic and avant-garde texts, constructed on a monologic consciousness, were difficult in principle. Postmodern texts, constructed on a dialogic consciousness, attempt to be as accessible and easy as possible. This is the position expressed, for instance, in Kundera's novel, *The Unbearable Lightness of Being*. Modern and avant-garde art assumed its position squarely in the center of culture, from which point it aggressively denied the reader's habits and needs. Following the death of Utopia, postmodern art found itself on the fringes of culture, from where it was forced to lure back its readers, who had been bewildered and stunned by modernistic and avant-garde provocation, and had consequently surrendered to the simple clichés of mass media culture. This is how one of the principles of postmodern art emerged: self-referentiality. Postmodern art is replete with self-commentaries, immanent analyses, and post-analyses of the author's own text (Eco's essay, *In the Name of the Rose*), author's prologues and epilogues, notes and "glosses" (the Ovidian repertoire in Christoph Ransmayr's novel, *The Last World*).

Croatian literary postmodernism came about in two ways: former modernists, encountering the death of Utopia, became postmodernists—or else a new generation of writers, for whom the death of Utopia was an initial premise, emerged on the scene. In the first case, postmodernism developed in the isolated artists' workshops. The modern writer Ivan Slamnig, who had been known previously to quote verses and rhymes from other poets, became a zealous "citationist" and self-referential poet, marking his quotational encounters with the allusion "as the poet would say," and elucidating the title of his poem, *Dronta*, by referring to a notation from an encyclopedia. Antun Šoljan, a modernistic poet and the author of escapist prose in his youth, composed a referential spoof under the title, *The Croatian Joyce*, in which the author appears as the discoverer, editor, and commentator of a nonexistent writer named Šimun Freudenreich. Deducing etymological associations from the name of this fictional writer (Freud + Reich and Freuden = joys), Šoljan hails his nonexistent author as a Croatian Joyce and calls his masterpiece, *Smail-aga's Wake*, a Croatian *Finnegan's Wake*. The philologist and professional lexicographer, Tomislav Ladan, made the transition from modernism to postmodernism in one and the same text, the novel, *The Bosnian Crest*. The transition takes place in the second edition, for which the author wrote a series of ironic self-commentaries about his genre, his Bosnian subject, and the relationship between the author and the reader.

During these years, however, there was one place where post-modernism occurred collectively: in the small department of the Philosophical Faculty in Zagreb, the Institute for the Study of Literature. At the time of the Croatian Spring and immediately thereafter, a large group of young people were appointed to the Philosophical Faculty. At the time of the Declaration, they had all still been students, and at the time of the student movement and the "Spring," they had just completed their courses. Thus, they had taken no direct part in the Declaration or the "spring." Among those who had just been appointed at that time was the author of this tale; that is, the female character who had just returned from Vienna.

A complete divorce of culture from politics had transpired. On one side was CULTURE, and on the other, REPRESSION. Croatian intellectuals withdrew into their personal or collective internal exiles and founded their own realms of liberty, or at least the illusion of liberty. Culture became a well-protected preserve, and the best and most secure was the Institute for the Study of Literature of the Philosophical Faculty in Zagreb. It was in this preserve that Croatian postmodernism came into being as an original, spontaneous, and collective phenomenon.

Most of the young staff members who found themselves in the Philosophical Faculty and Institute were at the same time writers—

writing original literature—and literary scholars or essayists teaching literature and writing about literature. Dubravka Ugrešić taught Russian literature and wrote intertextual prose in which she played with the simple conventions of the love story (her short novel, *Stefica Cvek in the Maw of Life*), but also with the major genre of the epic novel (*The Fording of the Stream of Consciousness*), and even explained her own prose and intertextual works in the form of self-commentaries, notes, or glosses. Pavao Pavličić taught older Croatian literature, especially the periods of Mannerism and the Baroque, and wrote whodunits and fantastic crime stories at regular annual intervals ("like plants," he remarked in conversation). And I wrote a poem *American Scream*, which began with the lines:

> Poets are Indians. Verses
> Reservations

When I wrote these lines in the early '70s, I had not yet heard of the phenomenon of quotation, on which I wrote a study in the late '80s, *A Theory of Quotation*. But these lines were quotations, they were written on the model of lines by the modernist poet, A. B. Šimić, "Poets are a wonder in the world." The modernist, Antun Branko Šimić, has expressed in his lines a basic feature of modern and avant-garde art—the phenomenon of de-familiarization (a term used by the Russian Formalist, Viktor Šklovski, and subsequently in a quite different sense by Bertolt Brecht). I had expressed in my lines my personal situation, the situation of my group in the Philosophical Faculty, and at the same time the situation of poetry in postmodern culture.

The Third Part of the Story, or the Palindromic Apocalypse in Croatia, 1991

In 1968, the Russian tanks in Prague crushed the idea of Communism. In 1971, by suffocating the Croatian Spring, Tito killed his own idea of Yugoslavia as a community of fraternal nations and peoples. The spirit of Utopia had already died in those years, but the corpses of the states in which it had lived had not yet been interred. The burial of these defunct Utopias took place much later and under different circumstances. In 1989, with the fall of the Berlin Wall, the Eastern Socialist empire was

192

simply, and joyfully, buried. Two utopian superstates, the Soviet Union
and Yugoslavia, both born in the same year, 1918, at the height of the
avant-garde and modernism, were buried in the same year, 1991, at the
height of postmodernism. The Soviet Union was buried hastily and in
peace. At the United Nations on the East River, when the Soviet flag
was replaced by a Russian tricolor, the only witness was the wind. Tito's
Yugoslavia was buried in the blood and the ruins.

These events divided postmodern culture into two stages. Spontaneous,
implicit or aesthetic postmodernism lasted from the death of Utopia
until the burial of its corpses (1968–71 and 1989–91). After the funeral,
self-conscious, explicit or political postmodernism began.

In this record of events I shall permit myself a modest degree of self-
referential authorial freedom and consider a text of my own—a "poetic"
text. I am referring to *Palindrome Apocalypse*, which in a strange sense
had predicted the events in former Yugoslavia: 1991/ RIM I MIR / ILI /
ONO (1991 / ROME AND PEACE / OR / THAT).

The palindrome is an ancient, infantile, or magic linguistic game in
which all the words or sentences may be read from left to right, or from
right to left, backwards or forwards, from the East or from the West.
The best-known palindrome is the Latin formula in the shape of a magic
square: "SATOR / AREPO / TENET / OPERA / ROTAS;" in
translation, "The sower Arepo holds the cart with difficulty." Palindromes
were written by Mallarmé and by the Russian poet, Velimir Hljebnikov,
while the longest palindromic text on record was written in 1979 by the
New Zealand poet, Jeff Grant (11,125 words).

The first version of *Palindrome Apocalypse* was written by request for
a special issue of the *Osijek Review* (1981), which was devoted to literary
puzzles and riddles. The text bore the date 1991 in the title since this was
the only year in the twentieth century that suited the palindromic game,
i.e., that read the same from both left and right. The poem ends with
an airplane flying over the central square in Zagreb. The pilot asks his
controller whether he should drop his load, receives the go-ahead over his
radar, and the bomb falls on the main street in Zagreb, which is named
Ilica. Someone asks in astonishment in the Kajkavian dialect "KAAAJ?"
(WHAAAT?); someone else replies that it is true, that the fools have
dropped "ONO" (THAT), i.e., the bomb, and the poem ends with the
apocalyptic line: "O Romo—Gomoro" (Oh Roma—Gomorrah) and the
dispatch of a telex to the effect that a skeleton has been observed, and the

horror is worth seeing. This was conveyed in palindromic lines:

— KAAAJ?

Ilica?

Bacili???

A? Da–da…

O   N   O

I to idioti
A T O M   S M O T A
Nama aman…
Ata! Ata!
Romar—mramor
Oganj, ago!
Kisik! Kisik!
Nama—zaman
Teleks: »SKELET!«
(Roza razor…)
K A L
       B O L
          O B L A K

Idi!

Vidi!

(*Osječka revija*, 1981, 6, 72)

or, translated:

— WHAAAT?

Ilica?

They threw it???

Ah? Yes-yes…

T   H   A   T

And it's idiots
THE ATOM REELS
Please, save…
A horse! A horse!
Pilgrim—marble
Fire, oh lord!
Oxygen! Oxygen!
To us—in vain
The telex: "A SKELETON!"
(Pink destruction…)
S L I M E
PAIN
A CLOUD

G o!
S e e!

Ten years after these lines in palindromic language had been written, the event described here actually took place in Zagreb—on 7 October 1991. The Yugoslav generals bombarded the old town of Gradec with rockets, the governor's palace was demolished, Ilica shuddered, the inhabitants of Zagreb, sitting in their cellars, wondered what sort of idiots the generals were, and Croatia was transformed into Sodom and Gomorrah. Other lines from the Apocalypse also came true: in Croatia "grey Jesuses" really did "hang" ("I vise sivi / Isusi"), the "doorbell of Hell" ("Alka pakla") really did ring and "the Russian was rushing" ("Suri ruj i juri Rus")—in a Yugoslav bomber. Their former common fatherland that the guest-workers had dubbed "Jugo" was now apostrophized as "the serpent" ("Gujo").

I continued adapting the first draft of the poem from the *Osijek Review* and extending it until the time of the Chernobyl disaster in 1986. During those years I was shuffling words and sentences to see whether they were the same from both ends, and how they might be fitted into the poem. The work began to evolve on the intertextual basis of two Croatian epics: the baroque epic by Ivan Gundulić, *The Tears of the Prodigal Son*, and Ivan Mažuranić's neo-Classical epic, *The Death of Smail-aga Čengić*. The poem was divided, on the model of Mažuranić, into five cantos, and these were termed "Cries" (from the baroque term, "Laments").

The poem's subject was intended to be a voyage in time through the history of the twentieth century, from the October Revolution of 1917 ("CAR U KURAC!"—"TO HELL WITH THE TSAR!") to the palindromic disaster in 1991. In its central "Lament," "DER RED" (*DER ORDER*"), a metaphor for Hitler and "BRK SKRB" ("MOUSTACHE GUARDIAN"), a metaphor for Stalin, events succeeded one another with a precision that astonished and frightened me: the Second World War ("A b o r t u s   u t r o b a"—"A b o r t i o n   o f   w o m b s"), ("Minu punim"—"I fill a mortar shell"), the dividing up of the world at Yalta ("At laje—JALTA"—"A horse neighs"—"YALTA," "Tebi Tibet! / Nama Aman!"—"Tibet to you! / Amman to us!"), Tito's quarrel with Stalin ("Piso Josip / Sipo opis / Sipo popis"—"Josef wrote / Scattered a description / Scattered a list"), the creation and collapse of a Socialist empire ("MIR KOMUNIZMU! / Um zinu. Mokrim…"—"PEACE TO COMMUNISM! / Mind gaped. I urinate…", "Ruska tema: metak sur"—"A Russian theme: a grey bullet"), Russian tanks in Budapest ("Rađa Mađar / Katar kratak"—"The Magyar gives birth / To a brief catarrh"), the rocket crisis in Cuba ("A Kuba? JABUKA!"—"But Cuba? AN APPLE!"), the collapse of the Prague Spring ("UGAR PRAGU!"—"BLACK SMOKE TO PRAGUE!"), the collapse of the Croatian Spring ("Hrvata vrh"—"The summit of Croats", "NATO GETO TEGOTAN"—"THEN A DIFFICULT GHETTO"), the oil crisis ("Oseka, keso!"—"Low tide, purse!"), Khomeini's rise to power ("Omamo,/ i m a m"—"Oh stupor, / i m a m s"). At the end of the poem the author realized that the idea of the best of all possible worlds personified in the "Moustache Guardian" and the "a gray bullet" is to blame for it all ("UJEDI IDEJU!"—"BITE THE IDEA!") and found that the manneristic palindromic pun was the only proper language to express it ("Hocke, rekoh / Ore pero"—"Hocke, I quoth / The pen ploughs"). A problem arose in 1986, when the Chernobyl disaster occurred. This event actually coincided with the palindromic apocalypse in the lines, "Opor veo, Evropo!"—"A crude veil, oh Europe!" Then I became frightened of my poem and had no wish to publish it in its new extended form. I was afraid of its palindromic language, its truth. I threw it into a drawer and forgot about it.

It was on 9 January 1991, that the Yugoslav generals uttered their first threats; on 16 January, the Gulf War began. The citizens of Croatia turned out for a referendum, and 93 percent stated they no longer wanted Yugoslavia, but an independent and sovereign state. That infuriated the dead utopian octopus with its innumerable tentacles, and especially the well-fed utopian body of the Federal Army, whose soul was disintegrating and which was changing into a vampire in the process of dissolution. The day after the Croatian Parliament declared independence on 25 June 1991, the war had begun.

At that moment, for the first time since Chernobyl, I recalled my palindromic apocalypse. I hunted through the drawer and found all the versions, from the shortest to the longest. In each of its versions, the poem began with the line, "And grey Jesuses / Hang," and ended with scenes of an apocalypse in the center of Zagreb. I once again decided to leave it in my drawer. The killing and mass murder of innocent people began, Zagreb was flooded with refugees, and village churches were left without their belfries like headless people. That was just the beginning. I was ashamed of every word, every line. When lines noted at the end of the poem came true on 7 October, I was not thinking of the poem or of those lines. That day I rushed to the shelter eight times and stayed awake under cover until the early hours of the morning. I had more important things to do.

I didn't think of the poem again until the first days of 1992. I took it out of my drawer, and it no longer scared me. What the palindrome written in the Croatian language in 1981 had predicted for 1991 had already transpired. A horror film was playing in my mind, and I was wondering what my text had to do with actual historical facts in the real world of 1991. What does a year in the title of a poem have to do with that same year in actual historical time?

My answer was as follows: very little—and a great deal. The palindromic language is an utopian linguistic game. No one speaks it and no one ever will. Its basic principle is utopian; namely, it is identical from both ends, it reads equally well from left and right, from East and West. In normal language, normally aligned in space, there is a left and right side, there is East and West, and it never occurs to anyone to identify these two opposites. But it did occur to the palindromic language—and to me, the author of this poem.

While I was writing the poem I was living on an academic and aesthetic "reservation:" the Philosophical Faculty of the Institute for the Study of Literature in Zagreb. The utopian idea of one language with two varieties, "eastern" and "western," Serbian and Croatian, counts among my most deep-seated traumas, and during the period of aesthetic postmodernism, I reached out for the palindromic language. My painful experience of Serbocroatian linguistic uniformity transported me mentally to a global plane, a palindromic language in which both sides were the same. This palindromic, left to right, right to left, or alternatively, right-left or left-right, east-west or west-east language, however, was capable of expressing only one single theme: the APOCALYPSE. While I was writing the poem, I was thinking of the global antithesis of East and West, fearing that the atomic conflict between the two blocs that still existed at that time would begin with the dropping of a nuclear bomb on Zagreb. Fortunately, this conflict never materialized. No nuclear bomb from Moscow or Washington was ever dropped on Zagreb, but rockets from the Yugoslav Army were fired at the city. The circle was closed. Through an ironic game of fate, the metaphors were realized, and the palindromic apocalypse took place in my homeland.

The palindromic, left-right or right-left, east-west or west-east reading was nothing but an unconscious aesthetical processing of the utopian homogeneous Yugoslav Newspeak called the Croatian or Serbian, Serbocroatian or Croatoserbian language. The more aggressively the utopian idea of the absolute uniformity of left and right, east and west, Serbian and Croatian tried to impose itself, the more the Croatian language was bound to become Serbian, and the Serbian language Croatian; the more ferociously uniformity was imposed by force, the closer the apocalypse came. And it actually happened when one side, the Croatian side, said NO.

And so we return to Kundera's model. In Kundera's design and in the real-life tale of our protagonists, it was anonymous individuals who said NO to Utopia. At that stage, Utopia was able to maintain itself only by punishing the disobedient individuals: it ate its own children. In 1991, the citizens of the Republic of Croatia said NO to Utopia. The response was a war. Utopia was already dead and vampires in uniforms of generals appeared on the scene.

In 1991 Croatia, Kundera's model ended up as a bloody Balkan "joke." The dead Utopia no longer had anything to save or anything to lose. It could do nothing but kill, and that was all it wanted to do. The war in Croatia in 1991 is a palindromic apocalypse in which the dead Utopia is taking its revenge because the two sides, left and right, east and west, Serbian and Croatian, have not become one.

The author of this tale (that female character from Vienna of so many years ago) wrote the palindromic apocalypse in splendid academic isolation during the period of aesthetic postmodernism in the '80s. The dead utopian language in which both sides are the same was revived for a moment without my will or knowledge, so that it might itself predict the apocalypse of Utopia in Croatia in 1991. This self-commentary was composed in the first days of political postmodernism—1992. I wrote the final sentence on the night of 15 January 1992 while watching on television a series of announcements that the Republic of Croatia had been recognized as an independent state.

Zagreb, 15 January 1992

POETRY OF MANY HAPPY RETURNS

by Bernarda Katušić
translated by Sonja Bašić

Nalijevo krug
Nadesno krug
I krug na krug
Opet je krug

About face left
About face right
And about upon about
Is again a circle
(*American Scream*, text 62)

It is impossible to draw a clear line between the modernist and
postmodernist concept of art, especially when dealing with smaller
bodies of literature such as that of Croatia, which never achieved
the radicalism of the "historical" twentieth century avant-garde
movements. Croatian modernist poetry reached its peak only in the
late 1960s and early 1970s; a uniquely paradoxical time characterized
by the simultaneous affirmation and subversion of both modern and
postmodern aesthetic tendencies. One of the possible delimitations of
these two poetics lies in their concept and experience of language, at
the time when the avant-garde utopian project of creating a new social
order—the best of all worlds—by means of a new language, began to
lose its intensity. In contrast to the avant-garde, which represented the
apex of modernism in that it demonstrated the materiality of language
and deliberately exposed the processes of conventional meaning,
postmodernism sought out possibilities for new structures of meaning.
Unlike the avant-garde notion of "transmental language" (Russian *zaum*),
which assumed that the new language could reach areas of meaning
situated beyond everyday communication, beyond the vague and
ambivalent frameworks of shattered logic, literally among the "language
of the stars" (Velimir Hlebnikov), the postmodern movement stated
its open distrust in the power of language. Contrary to the modernist
concept of art as a way of establishing a fundamentally new relation
between the sign and the thing, the casting off of the old, "outworn"
mantle of signs, dressing it in a new uniform, the postmodern revives

the "dead" signs of civilization and focuses directly on the process of their erosion. By renewing traditional meanings and reviving those that are ostensibly hidden, the postmodern illustrates the impossibility of constructing a meaningful world with language, and demonstrates that the spaces situated beyond the clichés of speech are also ruled by mere empty formulae, just as ideological projects conceal the meaningless babble of the collective consciousness. By relying on avant-garde experiences, the postmodern concept unexpectedly turns them upside down, exposing the devices and processes by which meaning is loaded and then emptied, and revealing the underlying mechanisms and structures of meaning. At the very moment—which can never be precisely established—when one cultural matrix was exchanged for another, the project of radical change was replaced by a project of careless nonchalance; a pathos of deliberate destruction was replaced by the pathos of ludic abandon; the universal "language of the stars" yielded to the principle of intertextuality and parody; and the poetics of commitment gave way to the poetics en légère.

Although the postmodern writing of Dubravka Oraić Tolić was not completely postulated until her poetry collections *American Scream* (1981) and *Palindrome Apocalypse* (1993) appeared, in her first book of poetry, which bore the indicative title *Eyes without a Homeland* (1969), she was already revealing the devices of linguistic semiotic process and its magic power, trying to recapture the spirit of those who "both erase and place signs among sea weed, birds, and boats" (*American Scream*, text 5). She began as one of a group of young poets who, after their initiation into the postmodern, brought an entirely new concept of poetry into Croatian literature. Within the space of two years—from 1968 to 1969—almost all these new poets published their first books of poetry (Zvonimir Mrkonjić, Luko Paljetak, Zvonko Maković, Josip Sever, Branko Bošnjak, and Darko Kolibaš). At a time when a Communist mindset was still in force in Croatia, Dubravka Oraić Tolić was personally experiencing from exile what later became one of her leitmotifs: "Poets are Indians. Verses / Reservations." Living abroad, she chose to place herself in the position of a "weak subject" undermining the "strong" official ideological and aesthetic concepts in force in her home country. Countering the existentialist subjective poetics of her colleagues, the exiled poet produced her first collection of poetry, which she later modestly characterized in her book *Književnost i sudbina* (*Literature and Fate*, 1995), as "a collection of poems with a sentimental title, and full of refugee rhetoric," but in fact it already showed signs of what was to become her poetic vocation. The exiled poet was aware even then that poems—like ideologies and utopias, history and civilization, nation and homeland, the world in which we live—are nothing but riddles, parts of an endlessly spinning cosmos of signs (*American Scream*, text 57). Spinning without end the signs of culture, literature, ideology and life, these husks of "fragile words" no longer pretend to reflect the real, but, like shadows of invisible objects, are compared by the poet/theorist to "the Moon, revealing only one resplendent and clear side of her face" (*Književnost i sudbina*, p. 33). By questioning language signs as poetic material and theme, as an exposed system of signs, a form of communication and way of life, a means of alienation and domination, an instrument of mystification and deceit, clichés simulating and annihilating reality, the poet demonstrates that these are merely strategies used by a writer schooled in theory, who then employs them on her voyage into the vast regions of the universe to get "under the very skin" of the world (*American Scream*, text 40) in order to catch a glimpse of the other side of the Moon. An emphasis on the foregrounding of language is one of the main reasons the poetry of Dubravka Oraić Tolić has been compared to the avant-garde spirit of the beginning of the twentieth century.

Playing with Language

The avant-garde cry for the "New! New! New!" (*American Scream*, text 20) is the prime postulate of her poetic cosmos. By semanticizing language as material, but also radically liberating the lexeme, breaking down verse structure, using aleatoric syntactic constructions and alogical meanings—the expert poet/theorist alludes to identical strategies implemented by the historical avant-garde. For example, the letter "K" from the Croatian spelling of the name, "Kolumbo," becomes the protagonist in several of her poems, in the manner of early avant-garde linguistic somaticism. The play with the phoneme, the "C" in English and the "K" in Croatian, creates a semantic hot point not only in the title, *American Scream*, but in the entire poem. In the same collection, the Old and New Century are merged into two large letters C/K (text 79). In English, the "K" turned into "C" could thus be understood as playing this role in the title of the poem and the poem as a whole: Urlik Amerike translated as AmeriCan SCream, or in the definition of America/Amerika as 99 letters C/K (text 56). Other graphemes are also used in witty complex games, i.e., with the homonym ONO; the

"O" placed at the end of *Palindrome Apocalypse*, given the ambiguity of this palindrome, is transformed into a device which slows the process of meaning; in addition to presenting a challenge to linear reading, it also carries an "excess" of meaning by its reference to former Communist times, when ONO (Opće Narodna Obrana) was a slogan and name of the military civil defense organization. In Croatian, "ono" is also an indefinite pronoun: that. In some poems, the letter "O" functions as a cipher symbolizing mystery and zaum (transmental language) as $0 + 0 = 0$ (*American Scream*, text 57); in others, the geometric circumference of the circle. In the last lines of *Palindrome Apocalypse* the "O" assumes major importance: its shape is in direct relationship with the photograph showing a cloud of smoke rising from the Government office building, Banski dvori, in Zagreb, after it was hit by guided missiles in a bombing of the Croatian capital in the palindromic year, 1991. In text 89 of *American Scream*, there is an enlargement of the letter "T," which suggests a visual cross connecting America and India. In text 77 of the same collection, one finds "crucified Chris Tophor" both verbally and visually crucified on the letter "T." The relative pronouns how, where, this, and that transcend their functions and become centers of meaning in several texts. Here a poetic world is created by means of a new mythopoetic language in which the principle of aleatoric combination allows the poet to merge and fuse words unrecorded in any dictionary.

And yet, in spite of her avant-garde trappings, Dubravka Oraić Tolić is not obsessed by the need to create something "new" at all costs. Well-versed in literary and other diachronic aesthetic transformations in the arts, she deliberately erects an avant-garde poetic structure only in order to rock it, and then move confidently forward on her own feet.

Ali više ne u Novo
Nego sve više i više
U vjetar, krv i govor

But no longer into New
Rather more and more
Into wind, oratory and gore
(*American Scream*, text 63)

This mythopoetic language is not the typical "dada" or zaum, the broken syntagmas are not just empty babblings or ravings beyond the limits of communication. The newly coined words are composed of known and recognizable lexemes, colloquialisms, political slogans, media jargon, and culturological signs and symbols. The phenomena of literary mazes and combinations, the poetics of spinning and sudden turns, nonsensical games of palindromic language—all suggest an eternity of perpetuum mobile.

Čovjeku najdraža kugla glave
Zavrtjela se i još se vazda vrti
Kao da vrtnji nema kraja

To a person the dearest sphere of the head
Began to spin and is always spinning
As if there's no end to the spinning
(*American Scream*, text 57)

The poet's bright and playful spins and reversals, movements in circles, engagements in ancient and childish, magic palindromic language games, suggest that all words or sentences are identical regardless of whether they are read from left or right, forward or backward, east or west. Loaded with meaning, India is thus linked, i.e., to "indapitalism," Ariadna's thread becomes "Indiadna," idiot—"indiot," definition— "indifinition," incident—"indicent," and New York turns into "New-Moscow," and then "MY IND-YORK." At one point, one of the central symbolic names, Christopher Columbus, is multiplied into "Christaling Christophors" (*American Scream*, text 68). The same principle of palindromic spinning is applied to the poet's game with current phrases, officialese, political slogans, clichés from Marxist and socialist ideology, cultural symbols, images from collective memory, inherited texts, and life itself.

An example of this is her use of the word/image "star," one of the oldest symbols in lyrical poetry (irresistible even to the avant-garde; i.e., Hlebnikov used the term "language of the stars" to denote his utopian "newspeak"). The star, one of the most powerful cultural symbols, but also one of the most common poetic tools, also holds a central place in the poetry of Dubravka Oraić Tolić and is used in her ludic confrontation with the Croatian poetic tradition and poetic tradition as a whole, including the avant-garde. In the subtle lyrical pattern of *American Scream* and *Palindrome Apocalypse*, stars appear in biblical, renaissance, modernist, avant-garde, and postmodern contexts. The poet does not see them as eternal symbols in a romantic sense, does not stress their divergence from modernism or subject them to avant-garde experiments; but, rather, like a bright and playful Colombine (as she has been characterized by the critic, Zdravko Zima), juggles all these possibilities. In one poem, as if in ecstatic reverie, she exclaims: "And we rotate, rotate / Around the stars" (*American Scream*, text 42), in another, "Everywhere only stars are sown" (*American Scream*, text 62). Then, in a ludic move, she turns to modernist synesthesia for "the blood that here, look, trickles down the stars" (*American Scream*, text 5), in another quick turn, she constructs a truly avant-garde signum, "Vernally ploughs with the starriest shoulder straps" (*American Scream*, text 62). From the patterns created by her poetic spins, these stars often rise like postmodern lighthouses amid the immeasurable sea of meaning. Personified, revived, inscribed with new references, the stars are those of Bethlehem (text 51) but also "Indies that shine at night" (20), "multipoint" (50), "withering away" (33), "sneezing" (56), "freezing" (50)—and the poet informally converses with them as well (50). Named or unnamed, mute or loud, smiling or sad, real or artificial, the stars are always present in the poet's urbis and orbis, casting their eternal light upon the "other side of the moon" and further dark corners of the universe otherwise inaccessible to the human eye.

The Citation Game

In her ludic, poetic spins, the poet does not limit herself to games with phonemes, lexemes, idioms, political slogans, and signs and symbols of culture, but combines and evokes many more complex linguistic structures and literary conventions, historical styles, authorial idiolects, and inherited sign systems. For example, *American Scream*, with its "round" structure (100 poems, 1 + 99), corresponds directly with the two greatest poetic works of western civilization, and the harbingers of the New Age—Dante's *Divine Comedy*, and Baudelaire's *Les fleurs du mal*, both of which trumpeted the arrival of modern lyrical poetry. In *Palindrome Apocalypse*, Dubravka Oraić Tolić also creates a direct dialogue with two of the greatest Croatian national epics: the baroque *Tears of the Prodigal Son* by Ivan Gundulić, and the neo-classical epic *The Death of Smail-aga Čengić* by Ivan Mažuranić. Her circular poetic world is intertextually interwoven with the visible and invisible texts of others, becoming a linguistic conglomerate drawn from a wide variety of sources. Voices and world views from the Bible, Homer, Xeno, Nietzsche, Kant, Hegel, Dante, Gundulić, Mažuranić, A. B. Šimić, Krleža, Tolstoy,

Gogol, Majakovskij, Mandelstam, Dreiser, Ginsberg, Queneau, Zajc, Lehar, Archimedes, Duchamp, Columbus, Vespucci, Marx, Tito, Stalin, and others are not mere ornaments, but elements overtly and covertly threaded into fictive textures and deliberately refashioned for new readings. In unexpected turns and combinations, the texts (quoted or unquoted), with their layers of meaning, speak for themselves in mutual juxtaposition, superimposition, and obliteration. The author often discards the role of poetic creator, becoming an integral part of the text, a playful composer participating in the vibrations of her intertextual score. The assimilation of other marked and unmarked voices is not simply a neutral synthetic process, but a constantly interrupted, deliberately syncopated echo of her personal aesthetics. In these poems, avant-garde poetic strategies are markedly postmodern: utilizing old poetics to create new ones, submitting an avant-garde vision to postmodernist inversion, replacing the zaum with the palindrome, and the poeta vates with the poeta ludens. In this ludic, circular movement, all the sides are always both up and down, left and right, in the West and in the East, overt and covert, new and old, and all extremes have been processed and muted, all artificial extremes subjected to obliteration. In this intertextual constellation, where the text is created by playing with quotations of existing texts, and its core circumscribed by a pliant and fluid circle, the author deconstructs former semeiological and semantic layers of meaning, confronts and dismantles the fixed, invisible, stereotypical, and long dead models of living and thought.

The Name and the World

By entering into the discourse, exposing the sign, searching for real meaning, Dubravka Oraić Tolić goes beyond playing with language and textual contexts. Although reality and the notions of home, country, people, nation, and life itself permeate her poetry, the thematic weight does not rest on the semantic deconstruction of concrete geographical-historical localities, but on their empowerment through words, metaphors, and symbols as elements of the text and culture. In a fictive letter addressed to the Ambassador of the United States of the Republic of Croatia in the 1990s, Peter W. Galbraith, she reflects on the motivation of *American Scream*, and explains the name of the word America and her "playing" with it as the "basic idea" of her poem:

I can't say for sure when and why I took the name of your country for my poem's theme. I can only say that it was the basic idea of my poem. The word "America" was never at any moment or phase of writing meant to be seen as the real country America represented by you in my country today. I was actually playing with the name of your country in the tradition of modern lyrical poetry: it was its fundamental idea, it is found in the title of the book and on all its pages. In my book "America" was always—a symbol, a metaphor.

American Scream is semantically modeled as an enigma of name detection, a lyrical riddle seeking an answer to the question: What is America? What is the content of the name of this symbol, which is meant to represent modern reality? What is hidden behind the name of one of the central archetypes of modern civilization? In a narrative structure shaped as a non-linear continuum, a lyrical web of dynamic (re)turns resembling ping-pong balls and their tireless movement up-down, down-up, left–right, right-left, childishly naïve, contrasted meanings are simultaneously affirmed and negated. In it, diverse points of view and contrasting notions of the name America, which was discovered by sheer chance and named the New Continent, alternate palindromically at a vertiginous speed, the known sides turning and spinning endlessly. The thematic starting point suggested in her fictive letter, that this name "never at any moment or phase of writing represented America as a real country" reappears explicitly stated several times in the poem.

Amerika nisu Sjedinjene Države
I ne zaprema 9 363 123 km^2 i nema 221 894 548 stanovnika
Amerika nisu Mountains s isklesanim likovima
    Washingtona, Jeffersona, Roosevelta i Lincolna
Ni slapovi Nijagare ni najveća tvornica automobila u Detroitu
Amerika nije *Deklaracija o nezavisnosti* iz 1776.
Ni predsjednik ubijen u kazalištu
Ni predsjednik ubijen u Dallasu

America is not the United States
And doesn't occupy 9,363,123 km^2 and doesn't have 221,895,548 inhabitants
America is not Mountains with the chiseled visages
    of Washington, Jefferson, Roosevelt and Lincoln

Nor Niagara Falls nor the biggest automobile factory in Detroit
America is not the *Declaration of Independence* of 1776
Nor the president killed in the theater
Nor the president killed in Dallas
(*American Scream*, text 18)

The same "negated" concrete geographical, historical, and political data of
the New Land, are then unexpectedly palindromically reversed, and, in
text 28, the name of "the discovered" India is used to denote the concrete
geographic affirmation of the avant-garde idea of the newest and best of
all worlds, and the "realized" metaphor of the discovery of the new, best
land.

> *U najboljem kraju*
> *Ili ostvarena Indija*

Najbolje se živi u najboljem kraju
Nikakvih problema tu više nema
U najboljim šumama najbolje ptice pjevaju:
Ovo je najbolje od svih vremena

U najboljem kraju najbolje je biti građanin od oka
Ljubljen od rijeka, ziban od vjetra
Gledaš s visoka na sve što teče
Nad tobom nadgradnja, pod tobom baza
Nijedna pustinja nije bez oaza

Učitelji tvoji počivaju u miru
Na najboljem zidu, u najboljem okviru
I sada se raduju i tebi i meni
Zadovoljni, sretni, dobri i rumeni

> *In the best land*
> *Or India's happy end*

In the best land the living is best
All the problems are laid to rest
In the best forests the best birds nest

211

Of all the ages this is the best

In this best land it's best to be
A citizen approximately
Beloved of rivers, swung to and fro
By the wind, you look from on all below
The superstructure above, below you the basis
There is no desert without an oasis

Your teachers repose in peace
On the best wall, in the best frame
And now they rejoice for you and for me
In satisfied, happy, red-cheeked fame
(*American Scream*, text 28)

But within the circles traced by the poems' turns and inexplicable
differences, America, "the land of dreams," the rich and happy land in
which freedom and liberty were achieved, is also seen from its other side.
Elsewhere in the same poem it is explicitly stated that America does not
always have "a smiling face" and does not come only "in the name of the
freest freedom," and thus has not "achieved" the utopian vision of a newly
discovered Promised Land.

Amerika je kao dijalektika
        U njoj je urlik kao što su u dijalektici
        I ja, i let, i klika

Amerika je strah i trepet
        Nasukanih pjesnika

Pjesnici, isprebijanih rebara
        Leže u pijesku:
        U krvi pjesme

        I kopna se lome

America is like dialectics
        A cry lies in it just as dialectics
        Hold I, and sky, and die

America is the fear and trembling
    Of stranded poets

Poets, with broken ribs
    Lie in the sand:
    In blood of poems

    And the shores shorten
    (*American Scream*, text 1)

In the lyrical web of these "contradictory" sides, as in the popular Rubik's cube whose elements can create a series of innumerable combinations, one can find the question of naming revealed and exposed from a childish point of view. Thus, in text 35, which is structured like a typical classroom riddle, the lyrical subject masquerading as a naïve teacher asks an equally naïve pupil to offer a definition of America. However, the naïve answer is more than ambiguous: America is "the land of dreams which every day begins with screams." The strange ping-pong play with meaning also reappears in text 37, where the definition of text 35 is changed into an "indefinition" of the New Continent:

Amerika—zemlja između zbilje i sna
I sve su manja i manja naša imanja
I sve je veća i veća
Američka sreća:
VREĆA BEZ DNA

America—the land between reality and dreams
And our estates grow less and less
And greater and greater is
American happiness
A SACK THAT LACKS SEAMS
(*American Scream*, text 37)

"A sack that lacks seams" (37) versus "sheaves of fear" (16); "the land of dreams" (35) versus "darkness" (16); a land of "satisfied, happy, red-cheeked fame" (28) versus "frightful land / land of fear" (14); "brutal, black (9) versus "too clean" (9). America is "like dialectics" (1), "like a bitter glass of spice" (9) which "blows like the wind / And collapses like fool's gold justice" (99). America is a lie (9), it is a "siren" (13), "America changes together with us" (65).

Amerika—to smo svi mi
Gdje god bili
Što god učinili

Amerika je ono što se rađa
Iz naših snova bez našeg znanja
Amerika je ono što nam se događa
Na putu prema Indijama

We are all America
Wherever we may be
Whatever we do

America is what is born
From our dreams without our knowing
America is what happens to us
On the way to Indias
(*American Scream*, text 18)

A možda je Amerika ovo:
Krik do krika i opet ab ovo
Novo! Novo! Novo!
Najnovije Novo,
       čovječe Božji
Amerika je način na koji se množiš

But maybe America is this too:
Scream to scream and again anew
New! New! New!
The very newest new,
       my good man
America's the way you multi-plan
(*American Scream*, text 20)

In the poetic world of Dubravka Oraić Tolić, the name America is
much more than a semantic focus or a signifying motor propelling
the poem and the book. Discovered by chance, given the wrong name,
sought as India, found as America, it offers itself as the coded sign of a

perfect model for the simulacrum as postulated by Baudrillard. It is like Disneyland, "a child's frozen world," where values are mummified and gift-wrapped in nonexistent kindness and warmth. In his famous essay *The Hyperreal and Imaginary* (1977), the noted French theorist described the real world of children's dreams as a miniature simulacrum of the real America; so also does the Croatian poet, starting from the name America as the real scenario for an imaginary dreamland. Just as Disneyland, as an inner space, has been contrasted to the world outside, and the infantilism of children to the adult world, creating the impression that the world outside is the real world (impervious to infantilism), Dubravka Oraić Tolić, true to the same principle, uses the name America to suggest a reverse system, a reversed infantilist constellation. In her deliberate staging of splendor, smiling dwarfs, and lovely princesses (identical to her aesthetic elaboration of the name America), the poet tells us reality lies in the world outside, where there are no fluorescent lights or magic beings, no staging, and no infantilism. But just as Disneyland is not solely an objective profile or a perfect reflection, but also an ideal copy of a contradictory reality concealing something else (a kind of ideological grid hiding the ideology of a third order, a microcosm of America existing only to emphasize the fact that the real America is itself only a vast Disneyland), America also becomes for Dubravka Oraić Tolić a model of a reversed reality, the crown of a sign-game with illusions and phantasms. Just as Disneyland is neither real nor imaginary, but a perfect scenario of a certain fiction of reality, the name America is a real grid, functioning as an ideal example of the ways that meaning is created and emptied, the deep mechanisms and structures that create thought as well as life.

In spite of her deliberately avant-garde trappings and her complex and ambiguous treatment of America as a New World, the best of all worlds, the poetic world of Dubravka Oraić Tolić does not respond to the notorious modernist clamor for the "New! New! New!". Playing with her palindromic, circular language, with its diachronic and synchronic signs of culture and life, the poet does not squander her aesthetic powers in building a New World and New Man, but by doing the palindromic reverse: restoring and reconstructing existing linguistic conglomerates in order to reveal her own circular orbit, the "totems of total man." The dark and visionary Cassandra, disguised as a playful Colombine, employs her sense of aesthetic restraint and linguistic measure to illustrate that the world is nothing but a labyrinth of signs swarming with one-way streets, and that modern man, crucified on the letter "T" like ChrisTophor,

215

is merely a sign emptied of meaning, a blinded child of Disneyland, seduced by magic beings, fluorescent lights, treacherously gift-wrapped totems, and symbols. Behind the language play, nonsense phonemes, lexemes, symbols, ideas of life and fate, the contemporary homo signum emerges at the point where all signs intersect: living and dead symbols, written and repressed texts, dreamt and transcended ideologies, actual and refuted taboos, forgotten and reborn ancient totemic images driven by the wheel of eternity in which everything is merged. "Play has crossed its categoric limits taking its own existence as reality" (*Književnost i sudbina*, p. 80), games with words have turned into games with fate, fiction has merged with reality.

(Jedna od niza
Mogućih posljednjih želja)

Please, odsijecite mi jezik
I bacite ga mačkama
Vjetar goni riječi
Prema mrtvim zvijezdama

(One of a series
Of possible last wishes)

Please, cut off my tongue
And throw it to the cats
The wind drives words
Towards the dead stars
(*American Scream*, text 98)

About the Author

Dubravka Oraić Tolić, poet, essayist, and literary theorist, was born 1 August 1943, in Slavonski Brod, Croatia. She studied philosophy and Russian language and literature in Zagreb, Croatia and Vienna, Austria; obtaining a doctorate with her dissertation on the phenomenon of the citation in literature and art. Since 1971, the author has been a member of the Philosophy Faculty, Institute for the Study of Literature at the University of Zagreb and, since 1998, has taught literary theory in the Department for Slavonic Languages and Literature. She has published numerous articles in Russian, which have appeared in the journal *Russian Literature* (Amsterdam). Her book, *Das Zitat in Literatur und Kunst* (*The Quotation in Literature and Art*), was published in the German language by Böhlau Verlag, Vienna in 1995.

Books in Croatian: *Oči bez domovine* (*Eye without a Homeland*, Zagreb, 1969); *Pejzaž u djelu A. G. Matoša* (*The Landscape in the Writing of A. G. Matoš*, Zagreb, 1980); *Urlik Amerike* (*American Scream*, Zagreb, 1981); *Teorija citatnosti* (*Theory of the Citation*, Zagreb, 1990); *Palindromska apokalipsa* (*Palindrome Apocalypse*, Zagreb, 1993); *Književnost i sudbina* (*The Literature and the Destiny*, Zagreb, 1995); *Paradigme 20. stoljeća* (*Paradigms of the Twentieth Century*, Zagreb, 1997); *Dvadeseto stoljeće u retrovizoru* (*The Twentieth Century in the Rearview Mirror*, Zagreb, 2000); *Muška moderna i ženska postmoderna* (*Male Modernism and Female Postmodernism*, Zagreb, 2005).

ACKNOWLEDGMENTS

Ooligan Press takes its name from a Native American word for the common smelt or candlefish, a source of wealth for millennia on the Northwest Coast and origin of the word "Oregon." Ooligan is a general trade press rooted in the rich literary life of Portland and the Pacific Northwest. Founded in 2001, it is also a teaching press in the Department of English at Portland State University. Besides publishing books that honor cultural and natural diversity, it is dedicated to teaching the art and craft of publishing. The press is staffed by students pursuing master's degrees in an apprenticeship program under the guidance of a core faculty of publishing professionals. By publishing real books in real markets, students combine theory with practice; the press and the classroom become one.

The following Portland State University students completed the primary edit, design, and market effort for *American Scream: Palindrome Apocalypse.*

WORKGROUP MEMBERS
Project management: Beth Dillon, Olivia Koivisto
Cover design: Kevin "Vinnie" Kinsella
Interior design: David Cowsert, assisted by Olivia Koivisto
Senior editors: David Cowsert, Linda Meyer
Assistant editor: Meredith Norwich
Proofreading: Olivia Koivisto
Marketing: David Cowsert, Olivia Koivisto

Linda M. Meyer

OTHERS WHO HELPED WITH *American Scream: Palindrome Apocalypse*
Susan Applegate   Lake Boggan
Jonah E.R. Loeb   Leslie Royal

EXTEND THE PLEASURE

Want more? Explore our website, courtesy of Zuri Media. Find out more about this book, and the others in our Croatian series: *The Survival League*, a collection of short stories by Gordan Nuhanović, and *Zagreb, Exit South*, a novel about discovery in midlife by Edo Popović. To access the Enhanced Book features of this book, return to the copyright page and follow the instructions for licensing this copy with Zuri Media.

ORDERING INFORMATION

Ooligan Press books can be found in independent, online, and chain bookstores in the United States and Canada

Ooligan Press titles are distributed to the trade by Consortium Book Sales and Distribution, 1045 Westgate Drive, Saint Paul, MN 55114-1065 (800/283-3572 or 612/221-9035) and are carried by all major book wholesalers and library jobbers.

Ooligan Press
PO Box 751
Portland, OR 97207-0751
www.publishing.pdx.edu

Colophon

This manuscript was set in Adobe Jenson Pro. Chapter openings are set in Gills San Std and Myriad Pro, while other headings, including canto numbers, are set in Lithos Pro.

It was printed on pH-balanced paper, and produced in Adobe InDesign CS2 with graphic work from Adobe Photoshop CS2.